"Maurice Sykes offers the unique perspective of a leader ι
icy, administrative, and practice levels, and across the boundaries of early childhood development, K-12, and higher education. Leaders with the qualities and skills that Maurice outlines are badly needed in today's challenging education environment."

MARTIN J. BLANK, PRESIDENT, INSTITUTE FOR EDUCATIONAL LEADERSHIP

"A fascinating story of the search for meaning in professional leadership. Maurice has told his story with such clarity and passion that it will energize young readers to aspire and help oldsters reexamine their own commitment."

BARBARA T. BOWMAN, IRVING B. HARRIS PROFESSOR OF
CHILD DEVELOPMENT, ERIKSON INSTITUTE

"Maurice Sykes has written an incredibly important book about the need for leadership in early childhood education. He rightly suggests that the benefits of investing in young children will not be fully realized without investing in a training and development strategy that builds highly effective leaders to support our early childhood education system. Our business leaders at the Committee for Economic Development understand the importance of training and that developing leadership skills is a key ingredient to the success of any enterprise. Our children deserve nothing less."

MICHAEL J. PETRO, EXECUTIVE VICE PRESIDENT,
COMMITTEE FOR ECONOMIC DEVELOPMENT

"Building the quality of the early childhood workforce and developing competent leaders is one of our greatest challenges. Maurice's voice is clear and strong as he outlines a set of core principles that serve as a roadmap to successful and enlightened leadership. In this autobiographical blueprint, he takes us through the journey of his own evolution as a thought leader while reminding us of the social justice basis of our work and challenging us to continue cultivating leadership abilities in ourselves and in our colleagues. It's a must for novices as well as for those more seasoned in the field."

JACQUELINE JONES, FORMER DEPUTY ASSISTANT SECRETARY FOR
POLICY AND EARLY LEARNING, US DEPARTMENT OF EDUCATION AND
FORMER ASSISTANT COMMISSIONER, DIVISION OF EARLY CHILDHOOD EDUCATION,
NEW JERSEY STATE DEPARTMENT OF EDUCATION

Doing the Right Thing for Children

Doing the Right Thing for Children

Eight Qualities of
LEADERSHIP

Maurice Sykes

With a Foreword by Thomas Schultz, EdD

Redleaf Press®
www.redleafpress.org
800-423-8309

Published by Redleaf Press
10 Yorkton Court
St. Paul, MN 55117
www.redleafpress.org

First edition 2014
Cover design by Jim Handrigan
Interior design by Ryan Scheife, Mayfly Design
Typeset in Sabon and Trade Gothic
Printed in the United States of America

Library of Congress Cataloging-in-Publication Data
Sykes, Maurice.
  Doing the right thing for children : eight qualities of leadership / Maurice Sykes ; foreword by Thomas Schultz.
     pages cm
  Includes index.
  Summary: "This book provides a clear framework and a systematic approach to help early childhood professionals become more capable, competent, and effective leaders as they serve young children. It presents eight core leadership values—human potential, knowledge, social justice, competence, fun and enjoyment, personal renewal, perseverance, and courage—and shares stories to inspire and challenge readers as they guide the teachers and directors they work with" — Provided by publisher.
  ISBN 978-1-60554-296-6 (paperback)
  ISBN 978-1-60554-390-1 (e-book)
  1. Early childhood education—United States—Administration. 2. Educational leadership—United States. 3. Early childhood teachers—Training of—United States. 4. Early childhood educators—United States.   I. Title.
  LB2822.6.S95 2014
  372.210973—dc23
                              2014009007

Printed on acid-free paper   U15-05

*To my mother and father, Eloise Browning Sykes and Joseph C. Sykes, who
helped to shape and form my core values by teaching me one simple rule:
do unto others as you would have them do unto you,
but do unto your siblings first*

*So, to my sibs: Joyce Katherine, Greta Louise,
Joseph C. (aka Butch/Yusuf),
Lawrence Raymond, and Bruce Anthony*

Many things we need can wait. The child cannot.
Now is the time his bones are formed, his mind developed.
To him we cannot say tomorrow, his name is today.

Gabriela Mistral

CONTENTS

FOREWORD

Growing up, my standard breakfast was cereal with milk, and Wheaties was prominent in the rotation of options. Its slogan, "Breakfast of Champions," went hand-in-hand with the then-popular adage that "Champions are made, not born." I think most of us dream about becoming champions and, even when those dreams don't come to pass, we still love to cheer for heroes and we yearn to follow inspirational leaders. Books and films about champions in sports, politics, business, and social change are best sellers, because we want to know what makes these men and women tick, what sets them apart, and what secret strategies or special capabilities undergird their success.

Those of us who make our careers in early childhood education cherish our leaders too, whether they set the pace for us as advocates such as Helen Blank and Marcie Whitebook; policy leaders such as Joan Lombardi, Harriet Dichter, and the late Helen Taylor; or researchers such as Robert Pianta, Barbara Bowman, and Sharon Lynn Kagan. We're curious about them too. As we implement policies they develop, attend their keynote speeches, or read their writings, we wonder about how they became so productive and influential. How did they navigate their pathway to leadership? What would we learn if they invited us to watch them negotiate behind closed doors with legislators, governors, congressional staff, or cabinet secretaries? How they would advise us if we could persuade one of them to become our mentor or leadership coach? What if we could spend a day talking with them about their lessons learned from decades of leadership at the highest level?

The book you are about to read, *Doing the Right Thing for Children: Eight Qualities of Leadership*, answers these questions from the perspective of one of my all-time, top-10, favorite early childhood leaders, Maurice Sykes. I first met Maurice in the early 1990s when he served as director of early childhood for the District of Columbia Public School System, leading a system-wide effort to improve teaching and learning opportunities for more than 34,000 preschool-to-third-grade children.

Urban school districts are not the most congenial environments in which to create developmentally appropriate and intellectually engaging classrooms for young children: Superintendents come and go. There is unrelenting pressure to improve standardized test scores. And veteran teachers are skeptical if not cynical about the never-ending cascade of innovations and reforms. Making a difference demands a wide range of talents and abilities. You need to garner and shrewdly deploy money, get parents on your side, recruit credible and effective trainers and coaches, and manage your boss so that you can promote your vision amidst a cacophony of competing initiatives from the federal government, foundations, and private sector partners—all of whom are "here to help." Most of all, you need to persuade thousands of teachers and more than one hundred principals to buy into new approaches to engaging children in learning and building productive relationships with each other—when you don't have authority over personnel decisions or evaluation procedures.

Maurice met and overcame these challenges by designing and managing a host of initiatives around a common agenda for improving classrooms and teaching, including:

- An annual Early Childhood Leadership Institute for preschool, Head Start, kindergarten, and primary grade teachers and teacher aides
- Early childhood demonstration centers for teachers and administrators to visit and observe
- Ongoing professional development through a cadre of collegial consulting teachers
- Seminars for principals and teacher-led study groups on education reform issues
- A new observational child assessment system and new report cards
- Funding for new furniture, materials, and equipment for classrooms
- Partnering with researchers to study the effects of these reforms on children's learning and engagement in schooling

How did he do it? The answer, as conveyed in this cogent and thoughtful book, is his commitment to eight core values: human potential, knowledge, social justice, competence, fun and enjoyment, personal renewal, perseverance, and courage.

While many books about leadership focus on strategies for managing, persuading, and motivating other people, *Doing the Right Thing For Children* focuses on these eight values and personal qualities. They are an interesting blend of unabashed values (human potential along side social justice is not often seen). He also does not hesitate to challenge readers to invest in becoming highly competent and deeply knowledgeable about themselves, about other people, and about the art and science of early care and education. Perhaps surprisingly he also speaks for the importance of fun and enjoyment and taking time in one's career for ongoing personal renewal. But these are balanced.

So, dear reader, I leave you with a question: are early childhood champions born, or are they made? What do you think? My answer, as we are so prone to say in the early childhood community, is "both/and." As we learn in this book, Maurice's path to leadership was developmental. It includes mentors who supported and challenged him and a sequence of career opportunities at the District of Columbia Urban Teachers Corps, Tufts University, the US Department of Education, and the District of Columbia Public Schools, prior to his tenure with the Institute for Educational Leadership. He is also a prodigious reader, who peppers his speeches, conversations, and writings with references to child development, adult learning, organizational development, and a host of other topics.

At the same time, I believe we are gifted with a few early childhood leaders who truly seem born to be champions. They seem to be wired up with a unique blend of insight and innovation, social and intellectual intelligence, and the charisma and magnetism to inspire and mobilize other people. In my mind, Maurice Sykes is one of these special people, and I thank him for his dedication in writing this fine book to guide current and emerging leaders to follow in his footsteps.

Thomas Schultz, Director for Early Childhood Initiatives,
Council of Chief State School Officers

ACKNOWLEDGMENTS

A thank you goes to the children past and present who have inspired my passion for doing the right thing for children and to the many teachers and administrators who have informed my work.

I also want to thank all the people whose stories are woven with mine; pieces of their stories that have impacted my leadership story appear in this book. I have changed their names or blended them into composites to tell my story; but even so, I hope you know who you are and accept my thanks. I am grateful to my two mentors Gwen Morgan and the late Kathlyn Johnson Moses—they invited me to be a leader. Kathy McKeon, my dear friend and colleague of many years, first suggested that I had something worth sharing with others and that there was a book inside me—thank you!

To Helen Chang: You have been my thought partner who helped me to organize my thinking around the topic of leadership. My special thanks to Kyra Ostendorf, my editor at Redleaf Press, for her unwavering faith in my ability to produce a book and who patiently encouraged, nudged, cajoled, and pushed me to get it down on paper and who then skillfully provided guidance, questions, and suggestions on how to make it better. Finally, a special shout-out to David Heath, director at Redleaf, for his continuous support throughout this process, who also believed that I could but wasn't always sure that I would—thank you, David, for keeping the faith.

INTRODUCTION

Doing the right thing for children encompasses an array of transformational actions and beliefs. When you do the right thing for children, you champion every child's right to high-quality learning experiences. When you do the right thing for children, you believe in the inherent value of every child, regardless of background. When you do the right thing for children, you take action to ensure that high-quality, meaningful educational opportunities are provided to every child.

The Root of Doing the Right Thing

For most of my professional life as a leader in early childhood education, I have been guided by the discovery and expansion of my personal core values. These values are the qualities I write about in this book; I hope they resonate with you and inspire you to take them on as descriptive qualities for yourself.

My career began in the late 1960s as a classroom teacher in an all-boys, ungraded primary classroom in Washington DC. The students in my care were labeled "at risk" and "economically disadvantaged." Yet I was fascinated by the way they acted, and by the way they thought about things. Their views of the world and the way they created stories amazed me. They could give meaning to the most mundane occurrences, and their moral sense of right and wrong was absolute. There in that classroom, the first of my core values—human potential—took root and grew.

My subsequent experiences continued to encourage the evolution of my personal core values. Today, they have become the qualities that I hold to be true not only for myself, but also for the entire field of leadership in early childhood education. Since those early days, I have served as a center director at Tufts University Educational Day Care Center, a national policy fellow at the

Institute for Educational Leadership, as an urban education program analyst for the US Department of Education, as the director of early childhood programs for the District of Columbia public schools, and as the deputy superintendent for the Center for Systemic Educational Change for the same school district. I am now the executive director for the Early Childhood Leadership Institute at the University of the District of Columbia, an organization that provides professional development and training for early childhood leaders in the District of Columbia.

Through my work in these roles, my perspective evolved and the leadership qualities that I share in this book emerged. My story is, of course, uniquely mine, but the leadership qualities are for anyone who is committed to doing the right thing for children.

The Investment Perspective

Does it pay to invest in young children? This may not seem like a question that is relevant to the topic of leadership in early childhood education, but it is. Leadership of any kind takes place within the context of the times, and right now the country wants to know: Is there a quantifiable return to be gained from investing in early childhood education?

The answer to that question from a political, economic, societal, and even military perspective is a resounding yes. Yet, to make these gains a reality, leadership at all levels is required—from the president of the United States to classroom teachers and parents. An investment not only in children but also in leadership is required. Here is an overview of our context of the times:

In his 2013 and 2014 State of the Union addresses, President Obama represented the bipartisan demand for education for our youngest citizens. The president declared that high-quality early childhood programs serve as the building blocks for societal contribution. As such, he called for a series of new investments that would establish high-quality learning for children from birth to age five in this country. The president's voice isn't the only one calling for reform. Organizations across the country are verifying the critical link between children's early education success and their future ability to contribute to society, which ultimately strengthens the nation.

Leading economists have run the numbers. Their measurements for identifying early childhood education as a sound investment are based on a host of economic and societal benefits, such as workforce development, high-school completion, and reductions in children being held back in school. Nobel Prize–winning economist James Heckman found that for every dollar invested in early childhood programs, the annual return is seven to ten percent.

Military leaders also say that early childhood education is critical to national defense. As written on the website for Mission: Readiness, an organization of senior retired military leaders working to educate policy makers on the importance of children and youth development, "early education helps children develop curiosity, character, and social skills—all key leadership qualities needed for success in the military or other careers." The Mission: Readiness organization actively supports early education programs.

State and local economic planners have unearthed the same findings. As of 2011, over fifty-eight states and cities have completed economic impact studies proving that early childhood education is critical for children's later success in life; therefore, early childhood education is a strong investment for the country as a whole (to read more on this, see the report "Economic Impacts of Early Care and Education in California" by Jenifer MacGillvary and Laurel Lucia). High-quality early childhood programs are now seen as a priority, and public policy is shifting to support this.

President Obama crystallized these findings in his 2013 State of the Union speech: "In states that make it a priority to educate our youngest children . . . studies show students grow up more likely to read and do math at grade level, graduate high school, hold a job, form more stable families of their own. We know this works. So let's do what works and make sure none of our children start the race of life already behind."

President Obama proposed an early childhood reform agenda to improve the quality and quantity of early childhood programs. Instrumental to his plan are the provisions for state standards, a rigorous curriculum model, and well-trained, highly effective teachers who are well compensated. In November of 2013, the Strong Start for America's Children Act was introduced in the Senate. This act builds on the framework put forward by the president in his State of the Union speech—it calls for new federal-to-state grants designed to improve education for young children over a ten-year time frame.

If implemented, these reforms have the power to create a policy direction that would level the playing field among young children in a way that has never been accomplished in past government-backed education programs. Prior to this current context, most of the national education-related focus has been on

K–12 school reform, which was incited by the stinging 1983 report "A Nation at Risk" that addressed the state of public education. The report states: "If an unfriendly foreign power had attempted to impose on America the mediocre educational performance that exists today, we might well have viewed it as an act of war." This report triggered a wellspring of efforts to reform public schools, most of which resulted in few measurable returns on the billions of dollars that were invested in them.

All of this is not to say that the federal government hasn't supported young children before. In fact, the first widespread program to promote early childhood development was the Lanham Act of 1940, which created government-sponsored child care so that women could enter the workforce during World War II. After the war ended, so did the program.

Then in 1965, the Head Start Program, offering services to low-income children, was launched under President Johnson. However, that program targeted only one specific group of children.

In 1971, with huge numbers of women in the workforce, early childhood educators were elated by the Comprehensive Child Development Bill, which declared that child development programs should be available, as a matter of right, to all children regardless of economic status or family background. However, although the Senate approved the bill, President Nixon vetoed the legislation in 1972.

The early childhood education community has had its brief flings with reform, but now we have opportunities on a level never seen before. Our time has come, and we must seize the opportunity.

Early childhood education is now receiving the broad support it deserves. The current push can be a major step toward building a solid infrastructure that ensures that *all children* are provided with the opportunities to learn and the ability to grow and succeed in an ever-changing global society.

The Call for Leadership

This, then, is where you and I enter the picture. The context of the times is calling for an investment in young children. But that investment in young children will only pay off if we also invest in the training and development of early childhood leadership. The broad societal demand for early childhood education is propelling educators to become well-trained and highly effective leaders.

This book provides a clear framework and a systematic approach for you to become a more capable, competent, and effective leader of programs and schools serving young children. If you are a teacher educator, a principal, or an agency head, I hope this book will inspire you to mentor and guide the teachers and directors you work with. We all have a role to play in doing the right thing for children—by being leaders that provide and demand quality programs for all children.

This book is a culmination of my years of study of a variety of leadership systems along with my personal experiences. Most of all, it is based on the set of guiding principles and core values that took root while I was working with those boys during my first teaching job and that have been developed throughout my own leadership journey.

Discovering New Leaders

I have been privileged to sit at many tables of leadership during my journey. At these tables, I hear the same recurring chorus: "We are a table of graying leaders. We need to recruit some new faces to take our places." For a time I thought these laments were sincere, but as I returned to those tables meeting after meeting, the truth began to dawn on me. There were never going to be any new faces to speak of, only the same old faces, sitting in the same old places, singing their same old song of lament.

I realized pretty quickly that if something was going to be done to change that tune regarding new faces at the leadership table, it was going to have to start with me.

I didn't rise into a leadership role on my own; I had been given a hand up from a mentor of mine, Gwen Morgan. Gwen was already a leader in the field of early childhood education, and she had seen some leadership potential in me. The opportunity she gave me, combined with a range of other experiences, led me to realize that the early identification and sponsorship of potential leaders by accomplished leaders is a strategic approach to ensuring that a next generation of early childhood leaders are in the pipeline.

Throughout my career I have continually sought out cutting-edge thinkers and practitioners who could challenge and inform my thinking and my leadership practices. I have searched everywhere for fellow journeyers who, like me, were interested in deepening their understanding of the art and science of leadership.

Today I invite you to join me at the leadership table to make a difference in countless lives by changing the way we advocate for, care for, and educate the young children in this country.

Your Leadership Matters

If you're reading this book, I'm guessing that you are a new or continuing leader who works on behalf of children. At the very least, you are someone who cares about children, and this is no small thing. You are an agent for change. You view high-quality early childhood programs for young children as an antidote to social and economic injustice. You are open to a wide range of possibilities in terms of improving educational outcomes for young children, and you are willing to confront and challenge your previously held ideas about what constitutes leadership. You are open-minded and willing to be dazzled, amazed, provoked, cajoled, and stretched in order to realize your full leadership potential.

If you see yourself in the description above, you're in the right place, and it is the right time for you to discover the leader that is within you by developing the skills, knowledge, and habits of mind that you need to lead programs for young children.

You might feel overwhelmed by the idea of achieving reform in the education system. That's fair. Huge challenges and problems exist, and none of them can be addressed with a quick fix. Yet, it is still possible to turn things around.

I teach my leadership students that there is a difference between our circle of concern and our circle of control. We're always concerned about huge things, so our circle of concern is always larger than our circle of control. But that doesn't mean we're powerless. Oftentimes, we fail to take advantage of the circle of control that *is* available to us. The truth is we usually have far more control than we realize.

What you need is a set of leadership qualities that motivates you to become a relentless agent of change with the goal of doing the right thing for children. It's time to start translating your good intentions into actions that will bring you as close to your desired vision as possible. The qualities in this book are your guide to success as a leader in early childhood education.

Now is the time! You are called to action on behalf of young children. Read on, and empower yourself with the tools you need to do the right thing for children.

The Leader's Core:
You Are What You Believe

If your actions inspire others to dream more,
learn more, do more, and become more,
you are a leader.

John Quincy Adams

Leadership is more than a title. Too many people—myself included—have been in a leadership position and assumed that their position gave them an understanding of everything. To really be a leader, you need to understand that you always have more to learn. And you need to be willing to get your hands dirty to learn it.

My story about this is from my first year of teaching at the Washington DC school. I was totally ignorant to what a teacher does, and I was able to experiment with a lot of out-of-the-box teaching methods. My ability to pursue some of the progressive ideas at that time was due in part to the fact that I was part of a national cadre of idealists who were interns in the DC Urban Teachers Corps.

The DC Urban Teacher Corps was a part of a national movement that rose in response to a countrywide shortage of teachers. Its goals were "to attract and train young men and women to teach in inner-city schools and simultaneously to have them experiment with and develop curriculum materials appropriate to urban youngsters." The Urban Teacher Corps held the belief that reasonably intelligent men and women who possessed commitment, flexibility, creativity, and concern could have a significant impact on inner-city youngsters. Three of the Urban Teacher Corps's assumptions, which the District of Columbia public schools wrote in 1968, shaped the leader and educator that I would eventually become:

1. The Student: "Many inner-city youngsters lack the essential skills of writing, reading, computation and reasoning necessary for effective

participation in our society. The school, and not the student, his family, its income, or neighborhood bears the major share of the responsibility for this inadequacy."

2. The Teacher Role: "The teacher is the catalyst in the process of learning; the student, his family, [and the] curriculum are all contributing factors but it is the teacher who guides and directs the learning process."

3. Training of Teachers: "By totally immersing the trainee in the classroom from the first day of school under the close supervision of experienced teachers, theory is married to practice. Interns can discover for themselves what teaching is all about."

When I started out, I was not the official teacher of record. That title belonged to Mary Johnson, my master teacher and supervisor. I worked for a year under her thoughtful, creative, experienced mentorship. The other corps members and I were given loads of support, encouragement, feedback, and patience. I was fresh out of college and was eager to absorb everything my coach had to offer.

At the end of the year, I had an evaluation. Ms. Johnson wrote the following: "Mr. Sykes creates engaging, challenging, and intellectually stimulating activities for the boys who are in his care. He is right on the mark in terms of active learning and the robust intellectual engagement that we had desired when we first established this arrangement. However, sometimes it is difficult to distinguish Mr. Sykes from the boys he teaches."

At twenty-three, I was pretty devastated by the last part. Even though Ms. Johnson likely meant that last sentence as more of a joke, at my current age and with my cumulative life experiences, I view being seen as one of the boys I was teaching as the highest compliment that could ever be paid. I understand now that I went beyond the surface of teaching. I was on my own learning curve, and I wasn't afraid to roll up my sleeves and learn what makes children tick. That was the foundation that enabled me to become a lifelong learner of child, organizational, and leadership development. Real leaders need to be willing to reflect on their abilities and experiences. They need to get their hands dirty.

Who We Are As Leaders

We each are a composite of what we believe, how we understand things, and the actions we take. As a leader, it is critical that your core values—your guiding principles—inform your leadership beliefs, thoughts, and actions.

Everyone has a core set of values. It is important for you to identify and articulate your core values to yourself and be aware of how they influence your thoughts, words, and deeds. Even at an unconscious level, your personal values are always present and always influencing how you carry out your leadership agenda. Your leadership agenda is your personal plan for transforming an organization. Any strong agenda must include a powerful vision and message along with strategic action steps. All of these things are guided by a strong set of core values. To stay on track with your leadership agenda, you must frequently take stock of your plan by looking back, looking forward, and looking inward. Your core values are the tools you use to keep you on course and moving in the right direction.

Anyone who wants to be a leader in the field of early childhood education must first make a personal commitment to doing the right thing for children and, even beyond that, must be guided by a set of leadership qualities. Your values, beliefs, experience, and training inform these qualities. You can learn these qualities for yourself, and you can develop them in others as well.

Based on my experience and success in the field of early childhood education, I have identified a set of eight qualities that I believe will lead to your success as a leader. These eight leadership qualities are human potential, knowledge, social justice, competence, fun and enjoyment, personal renewal, perseverance, and courage. They are the heart of this book.

Together, these qualities form my core values, and I hope they will inform yours too. I do not want to dance around the truth and say that having just any set of qualities will make you an effective leader. That is simply not true. If you want to be an effective leader and bring about enduring change, these eight qualities of leadership are nonnegotiable. I view the absence of any one of these qualities as a fatal flaw in leadership. With time and practice, these qualities can become your core values—when they do, your skills and efficacy as a leader will flourish, and you will empower yourself to do the right thing for children.

The Leadership Journey

Once you embrace them, these eight leadership qualities will serve as your moral compass to guide your thinking and actions as a leader. They will be your conceptual framework for organizational change and team development. Thus, the eight leadership qualities are what I call the road map to leadership success. If you stay true to these qualities while on your leadership journey, you will always move in the direction of effective and inspiring leadership.

This chapter gives a quick overview of the eight leadership qualities. Then in subsequent chapters, I show you in more detail how the qualities have unfolded during my leadership journey in the field of early childhood education and how they have led to effective and lasting change on behalf of children and their families. I hope the stories culled from my thirty-plus years operating from my core values will engage and inspire you. I also ask you to apply these leadership qualities to your own situation—leadership that is motivated by these qualities always starts at the personal level before it can affect communities and organizations. You'll find that when you take action that is based on these qualities, others around you will pick up on the positive vibes that you emanate. As a result, your attitude will become contagious, and you will be an inspiring and effective leader and agent of change.

The Eight Leadership Qualities

1. Human Potential

The human-potential quality ensures that you as a leader do the right thing because you recognize the untapped potential of every child and adult. With this leadership quality, you see each child and adult as a capable, competent, and resourceful individual in need of coaching, mentoring, and emotional support. Adopting the quality of human potential ensures that you always keep the interests of young children at the heart of every discussion and decision. The human-potential quality reminds you that there are no limits to learning for children and adults, just as there are no limits to an individual's potential.

The human-potential quality also informs how you as a leader view and talk to others in the workplace. It even influences how you interview potential candidates who are trying to join your team. Because you recognize that everyone is capable of realizing his or her full potential, you see in others what they do not see in themselves. You encourage and inspire them to develop and evolve in order to achieve their personal bests.

I have an unwavering belief in every person's potential to rise above the obstacles in life. I believe that human potential is infinite and full of possibilities. I believe that all humans have the potential to grow and transform into incredible contributors to the well-being of our global society. Effective leaders need to have this same faith in human potential for both children and adults. Whether I am developing a leader or teaching a child, I believe that having a positive outlook regarding human potential is vital to unleashing the intellectual and social dynamism that makes each person special and unique.

Great leaders have incorporated this quality into their core values. They act upon their understanding that all people are capable, competent, and resourceful by digging deeper with adults and children to discover and develop what is below the surface. In most instances, leaders with this core value have the uncanny ability to see, nurture, and develop a person's potential gift. Some people may only see deficits or underdevelopments in certain adults as well as in certain children. However, effective leaders always look for what makes people tick. They look for every person's gift. They look for every person's greatness.

2. Knowledge

Leaders hunger for knowledge. They seek knowledge in a wide variety of academic and nonacademic venues, including disciplines such as science, mathematics, humanities, business administration, and military science, along with the grocery store, the barbershop, and the people they encounter in the street. Leaders read. Leaders research. Leaders are consumed with wanting to know more and to understand more. They continually seek knowledge so that they can better understand themselves and the world around them.

Four levels of knowledge exist for a leader in the field of early childhood education: self-knowledge, knowledge of others, knowledge of craft, and knowledge of leadership.

One of the fatal flaws of ineffective leaders is the absence of knowledge. Ineffective leaders do not know their own strengths and weaknesses. They are easily blinded by a distorted sense of self. Thus, self-knowledge and knowledge of leadership are critical to being an effective leader. Effective leaders know what they do well and what they do poorly. They utilize their strengths and compensate for their areas of weakness by building a dynamic work team that is diverse in its skill set and mind-set.

In addition, it is crucial for a leader to have a wide breadth and deep depth of knowledge of others and craft knowledge. How does seeking and having a wide breadth of knowledge of people and one's craft help someone be an effective leader? Well, just like the popular saying "You can't teach what you don't know," an education leader who understands the people he or she leads and has a wide breadth of craft knowledge is a leader who knows the ins and outs of his or her area of specialization. A good leader appreciates that not everyone needs to be lead in the same way. A good leader stays current and is knowledgeable of the latest research theories and best practices in his or her discipline.

Having this knowledge allows leaders to explore out-of-the-box thinking and to stay at the cutting edge of their field. I have seen firsthand that those being led want to follow leaders who are more knowledgeable than they are. People want leaders who inspire and motivate them to consider and entertain new possibilities—which requires knowledge. After all, why would anyone want to follow someone who knows less than they do?

I tell new and emerging leaders, "You have to be at the top of your game. You have to know what you know, why you know it, and where you got it from." In other words, "You have to know the rules in order to break the rules." This holds especially true within a leader's area of specialization. By having extensive knowledge of the discipline, leaders can break the rules because they understand the cause and effect of any action. These leaders also understand how far they can veer off the beaten path without causing problems.

3. Social Justice

By social justice, I mean the mitigation of social or economic disadvantages that certain groups face or bringing voice to the marginalization of individuals due to race, class, language, disability, or sexual orientation. Social justice is about fairness, equality, and the acknowledgment that some people start out in life with better opportunities than others do. Because of this, my stand on social justice is to try to be a mediator between the circumstances where one starts in life and where one ends.

My desire to advocate for social justice is one of the main reasons—if not *the* main reason—for my involvement in education. Education is a good strategy to promote social justice because education can be a great equalizer. In addition, once a person has an education, it cannot be stolen.

Thus, a knowledgeable leader works to further social justice by creating high-quality programs for children, principally for children from under-resourced communities in urban areas. The goal is to provide resources to people who historically have not had a fair chance to succeed academically, socially, or economically.

Good leaders strive to uphold social justice for all types of people. The eight leadership qualities in this book apply across the board with all people. However, furthering social justice typically involves giving a voice to those who are underrepresented or have no voice in the community.

And this isn't just for children. Great leaders strive to empower teachers and upcoming leaders by helping them see their educational work as the socially responsible actions of a good leader.

4. Competence

Competence is about what you do with your knowledge. It is knowledge put into actionable behaviors that become a part of your leadership practice.

Competence is related to human potential as well as knowledge. Without living up to one's potential and continuously seeking knowledge, a person cannot be a great leader. This is because part of being a great leader comes from having enough confidence in one's own potential and breadth of knowledge to take action toward a greater goal.

As mentioned under the knowledge leadership quality, a great and knowledgeable leader is always on the cutting edge of his or her field. A great leader knows the newest approaches to workforce or human development. A great leader knows what tools are available to help other individuals reach their full potential. However, great leaders also have the uncanny ability to take all of these winning qualities one step further—their competence enables them to translate theory into practice. They are able to push the agenda of doing the right thing for children forward by actually making things happen.

Personally, I have always valued competence. I believe that a leader must be at the top of his or her game to further social justice effectively. A leader must deliver high-quality programs for children and high-quality training for teachers and aspiring leaders. These are the acts of competence that have the power to effect transformational change for children.

5. Fun and Enjoyment

I often say in my speeches that if doing something in particular is not fun, then it is not worth doing. The same goes for leadership. Leaders should bring a certain amount of levity to the work that they do.

Being a fun leader means being energetic and enthusiastic. It means bringing awe and wonderment to the workplace. People often say to me, "You always seem to be so full of energy." And I say, "I have to be; a broken spirit cannot lift another broken spirit." No one is interested in following someone who is depressed or depressing.

Embracing this leadership quality also means being able to take a step back and laugh at oneself. It means acknowledging one's shortcomings (even in front of children or colleagues) and not taking oneself too seriously. Another aspect of being a fun leader is to bring fun to the workplace—to lighten it up. One of the best ways to do this is with good humor. Joy and enthusiasm are contagious, so it is important for leaders to be happy and upbeat.

Please note that I am not suggesting that you partake in fun and games all the time. A good leader must be able to recognize when a sense of urgency is necessary and when a sense of lightheartedness is appropriate. Sometimes, the work is serious. Yet, most of the time, I've found that people can accomplish tasks and goals while being playful and enthused by the work that they are doing. For a field that places a high value on play, I am struck by how "playless" we can be as we go about our collective work.

6. Personal Renewal

Personal renewal is the act of revitalizing yourself so that you are able to give your best to others consistently on an ongoing basis. The process of personal renewal is important to being a great leader because it is through self-renewal that a leader balances and manages the stress that is a constant in any position of leadership. Without a means of renewal, a leader risks falling into the valley of despair and hopelessness, thus rendering him or herself useless to the cause of doing the right thing for children. A great leader must be capable of personal renewal in order to quell the everyday inner conflicts that result from juggling multiple priorities. You must keep your eyes on the prize and lead from behind and in front.

Steven Covey, in his book *The 7 Habits of Highly Effective People: Powerful Lessons in Personal Change*, states that personal renewal occurs at four different levels: physical, emotional, mental, and spiritual. It is through these four dimensions of renewal that a leader is able to gather the wherewithal to reenergize their passion, vitality, and determination to do the right thing for children.

Engaging in personal renewal means having a balance in one's leadership agenda. By having a balance, I mean that effective leaders are able to step away from their professional lives from time to time to restore themselves through acts of simple enjoyment. Effective leaders are able to renew themselves through things that have nothing to do with work, whether that means taking a leisurely walk or listening to a bird sing.

Note that the first leadership quality of human potential is the faith that leaders have in others and the belief that all people can demonstrate personal growth, if given the right opportunities. The personal-renewal quality is the belief in oneself to live up to one's potential and the responsibility to restore oneself when needed.

7. Perseverance

It is a cliché, but it is true: if at first you do not succeed, try and try again. Perseverance is the ability to accomplish long-term goals or implement visionary ideas in the face of challenges and setbacks. Perseverance is a character trait of great leaders who persist and stay the course in spite of multiple obstacles that threaten their plans and desired outcomes. Very often perseverance and persistence are used interchangeably and while there are some similarities, persistence is a dogged determination to get something done—to achieve a goal, whereas perseverance is a dogged determination to get to a destination that is congruent with the leader's hopes, dreams, and aspirations. In other words, persistence is a strategy that leaders who persevere must employ. Successful leaders seldom give up; they persevere. They have the willingness and the ability to endure tough times, disappointments, and even failure without whining, quitting, or loosing sight of their organization's values, vision, and vitality.

Leaders who are able to demonstrate an unwavering dedication to their organization's values, vision, and vitality represent what I view as the Three Ps of Leadership—purpose, passion, and perseverance. By purpose I mean why we do what we do; passion is what shapes our purpose and provides dynamic energy to our purpose; and perseverance is the driving force that enables us to stay the course in the face of seemingly overwhelming odds. I believe that perseverance serves as the driver and leverage point for a leader's core values.

Some new and aspiring leaders exhibit self-limiting behavior and speech. They start a project, run into an obstacle, and throw their hands up and say, "Oh, this is not working. We had better give up the project."

Effective leaders take a different approach. They realize that to achieve something that is worth doing there will be obstacles in their pathway toward success. However, these leaders view their challenges as opportunities to learn, grow, and develop. They work hard to develop new strategies and new perspectives.

I like to think of an obstacle as a metaphorical steep hill that I need to climb. To be successful I must be persistent in building up the physical and mental stamina I need in order to persevere and conquer that hill. So if it appears that a project that I am working on is going awry, I must build up the intellectual, problem-solving stamina to make a midcourse correction in order to meet with success. I must exhibit a realistic, can-do attitude that comes from a sense of learned optimism, self-confidence, and the need to persist. In other words, I must persevere until I remove the obstacle and accomplish my goal. However, as I accomplish that goal, I am well aware that the stamina I've build up will be coupled with new stamina that I will need for the next steep hill I must climb.

8. Courage

Courage takes on several meanings for a successful leader. Courage means keeping in mind the interests of the people that you serve. Being a leader with courage means that you understand the importance of your organization's mission and that you are willing to take bold steps on behalf of that mission.

Great leaders must also have the courage to acknowledge what is missing from their organizations and even from society. With courage, they must confront workplace incompetence, the failure of educating all children, and an absence of social justice. Only then can they implement positive change.

Just as important, courageous leaders must be able to check up on themselves. To be a courageous leader, you must have the courage to confront yourself about your contributions to either the success or failure of an endeavor. My experience has taught me that showing courage means not automatically blaming others for a project's shortcomings. Rather, showing courage means looking at yourself to see how you factored into the equation. Courage means taking responsibility for your own actions.

Qualities of Action

These qualities come together to create the skill set that leaders in the field of early childhood education need. I encourage you to think about how each of these qualities resonates within you. Do you have a commitment to social justice but perhaps not the self-discipline to stay current on content? Or maybe you are no longer having fun at something that used to be fun.

Regardless of your unique situation, know that you can make a difference in the lives of children, their families, and the adults you work with. These leadership qualities—when taken to heart—will guide your way.

Human Potential

Never underestimate the power of dreams and the influence of the human spirit. . . . The potential for greatness lives within each of us.

Wilma Rudolph

I have always wanted to help people. However, I never wanted to get into teaching. This whole career path was accidental for me.

In the late 1960s, fresh out of college, I was on track to becoming a social worker. At the time, the whole idea of social workers was that they helped people to help themselves, and that's what I wanted to do. I had a bachelor's degree in sociology and a minor in psychology. As far as I was concerned, that was the direction I was headed.

Life took a turn after a semester-long internship at the VA Hospital in Dayton, Ohio. I realized that social work wasn't a perfect fit for me after all. I decided that I would do better as an industrial psychologist, and I was actually on my way to Cornell University School of Industrial and Labor Relations to pursue a master's degree when something unexpected got in my way: the Vietnam War.

I had no interest in the war. I found the concept of war very disturbing. Even before going to college, my experiences had all been around peaceful and respectful solutions of problems and conflicts; I even served as the president of the youth branch of the National Association for the Advancement of Colored People (NAACP) in my local community. Somehow it came to my attention that I could get a deferment from serving in the war if I were a teacher in an urban area.

And that was how I got into teaching. That was how I found myself, at the age of twenty-three, standing in a room full of inner-city boys ages four through eight in Washington DC. There are no accidents in life, and I had landed exactly where I needed to be.

There at that inner-city school, all of my romantic notions about social work were shattered. The boys in my charge were a group of children that society had already given up on, even though they were only a few years old. No one believed that they could or would succeed. But as I worked with them day after day in that classroom, I began to see things that the naysayers said shouldn't exist. There were glimmers of genius in each and every one of those young boys. It wasn't a question of catching flickers of hope here and there. These children had potential that no one had even begun to conceive of.

It was my job to create an engaging and intellectually challenging curriculum for these children. To do that, I had to be interested in the boys as individuals. I had to be aware of their developmental needs and the cultural and economic context they were coming from. I had to value all of that, and I had to offer them opportunities beyond the boundaries of their neighborhoods as well. This was right after the riots of 1968 following the assassination of Dr. Martin Luther King Jr., and the atmosphere in Washington DC—indeed throughout much of the nation—was charged. I did everything I could think of to bring balance into my students' lives, and I did that by giving them a range of experiences that I knew their counterparts from middle-income families would be exposed to. I took them to age-appropriate cultural events. I arranged with the manager of a fast-food restaurant for them to see and work behind the counter of the restaurant. Then I introduced them to the sights and sounds of Bill Martin Jr.'s literature. I taught them all the freedom and protest songs of the time, and every Saturday I took some of them out to play touch football.

The more involved I became with them, the more they fascinated me. They told me things I just couldn't believe. The way they interpreted what was going on around them and their sense of social justice baffled me. They had a way of looking at the world that was intellectual—almost academic. These children were not defined by the inner-city circumstances that they were born into. They could have been any group of children, from anywhere else in DC or the nation. They had views on how things worked and how things should be, and their ideas broke through barriers in my mind—self-imposed ones that came from societal beliefs regarding the lack of ability of children from a certain class to achieve at high levels due to their racial, ethnic, or economic status.

I give those boys credit for being the root of everything I know and understand today. In the end, my experience with them was a key factor in giving rise to one of my core values: the indomitability of human potential.

I saw the raw potential in those children, and that's when my gears began to turn. I began to wonder, what makes people tick? How can you maximize people's inner strengths and abilities to help them realize their hopes, dreams, and aspirations? I had always been curious about what lies beneath the surface of humanity. I had always wanted to delve deeper into understanding human development and the human condition. Those things had been at the root of my early desire to become a social worker. I felt called to help people reach their full potential, and as a new teacher at that inner-city school, I had unearthed the way in which I would achieve that calling.

What Is Human Potential?

I define human potential as the untapped and underdeveloped attributes, abilities, and ambitions that—once realized—can lead an individual toward personal greatness and success. Recognizing and working to draw out human potential is one of the first steps you can take when it comes to doing the right thing for children.

Dr. Martin Luther King Jr. often quoted a poem that is in sync with my core value of human potential. Dr. King spoke the following lines from the poem at a speech he gave at the Institute on Nonviolence and Social Change in December of 1956:

> *If you can't be a pine on the top of the hill,*
> *Be a scrub in the valley—but be*
> *The best little scrub by the side of the rill;*
> *Be a bush if you can't be a tree.*
>
> *If you can't be a highway then just be a trail*
> *If you can't be the sun be a star;*
> *It isn't by size that you win or you fail—*
> *Be the best of whatever you are.*

Douglas Malloch wrote that poem, titled "Be the Best of Whatever You Are," in 1926. The poem's title captures what I believe human potential boils down to. You can be whatever you want to be. But in the end, you have to strive to be the best of whatever you are. As leaders in early childhood education, it's our job to find that individual spark of genius in each and every child and adult we work with and draw it out.

And the work doesn't stop there. Leaders need to understand that human potential extends beyond people themselves. It includes the organizations and institutions in which they operate.

A recent conversation with a school director went like this: When I approached her to ask if she would consider teaching a course, she replied, "You know, I really hate this organization." "That's really unfortunate," I said, "because this organization is affording you the opportunity to do what you do." This director did not see the potential in deepening her connection with the organization she works at. Her negative attitude prevented her from accepting a leadership opportunity to be part of the potential of the organization.

The bottom line is that human potential comes from valuing the things around us. Our institutions factor into that equation too. But in the end, our fellow human beings are the greatest resource that we have, and they deserve all the resources for development that we can give them.

Equalizing the Playing Field

One of the big things holding back potential leaders in our field is the misguided idea of leadership hierarchy. Too many people in leadership positions think, *I'm in charge of you, he's in charge of me, and there's no reason for any of us to mingle with those people way down there at the bottom of the ladder.*

There is ego, and then there is heart. Ego drives what you do as a leader that is centered on yourself. Heart drives what you do as a leader that is centered on others. A lot of leaders—in our field and others—make decisions or take actions based on their egos. They only want to be around people who think like they do, who act like they do, and who had the same kinds of experiences as they did growing up. But when we limit our minds and our actions to what we *think* other people can do, we lose out. We become indifferent toward other people's potential. I often say to underperforming teachers, "For all you know, the cure to cancer might be in that child's mind. But because of the way you are interacting with him or her, it will never be realized."

The truth is that you can't discard people just because they're higher, lower, or different from you. I learned this lesson from my mother when I was ten years old. Ours was a working-class family of eight—six children and two parents—in upstate New York. We lived in Lincoln Heights, a housing complex of attached row houses that was built to provide affordable housing for people who were working to support the war efforts during World War II. My brothers, my sisters, and I all had chores to do, and it was made clear to us that the chores were our contribution to the cohesiveness of the family unit. Now and then, however, my mother would hire people to assist with major chores like ironing or sizable cleaning projects.

There was a man who used to wash the interior walls of our house for us. He went by the nickname of Preacher, and he was really the handyman in our community. And I admit it, I looked down my nose at him a little bit. Our family wasn't high on the social ladder in the first place, so in my mind anyone who was below us must have been really washed up.

One evening after he'd finished washing our walls, my mother invited Preacher to join us for Sunday dinner. When he walked into the kitchen, he was filthy from the work he'd been doing. His clothes were dirty and drenched with sweat, and his hair was a mess. He smelled awful. But my mother sat him right down at our dining table, and we passed around the plates.

I didn't say anything, but I couldn't keep the expression of disapproval off my face. My mother noticed. After dinner, when Preacher had taken his leave, she pulled me aside.

"Don't you feel like you're better than him," she told me sharply. "Everybody has value. You can learn something from everyone."

I was skeptical that you could learn something from *everyone.*

"Yes, everyone," my mother insisted. "Even a fool has something to teach you, if nothing more than how *not* to be a fool."

She was right, and that was the moment that concept hit home for me. Before that, it had been a notion. I grew up going to Sunday school and learning the golden rule and everything, but all of that happened in abstraction. This man Preacher was a real person. When he sat at our table and ate our dinner with us, he talked about interesting things. But I hadn't paid attention to any of them, because I was too busy dwelling on my concern that he shouldn't be there.

The lesson I learned that day—that I can learn something from anyone—continues to be at the center of what it means to me to see the human potential in everyone. To be a good person, and indeed to be a great leader, you need to be humble yourself. But more than that, you need to look beneath the surface of other people. People are complex, and their lives are complex. And if you jump to hasty conclusions about them, you're missing opportunities. There are moments of enjoyment and even of greatness that slip through the cracks when you don't pay attention to each person's real and potential contributions.

People around the world are guilty of sorting and selecting and pigeonholing one another. It's almost instinctual for us to want to classify the people we meet and know. That's a habit we have to break as leaders—the sorting and selecting of people based on exterior attributes needs to stop. Current leaders have to give people the chance to live up to their personal greatness, to become leaders. To be a great leader, you have to be willing and trusting enough to go beneath the surface, and discover what is waiting underneath.

Good leaders know how to value all human beings.

Valuing Human Potential in Children

The child is "rich in potential, strong, powerful, competent, and, most of all, connected to adults and other children." This is a powerful vision of children written by Loris Malaguzzi in the November 1993 issue of *Young Children*, the journal of the National Association for the Education of Young Children (NAEYC). Malaguzzi was the founder of the internationally acclaimed infant-toddler centers and preschools of Reggio Emilia. His vision of the child is one that resonates for me, and it has inspired many early childhood educators to do the right thing for children.

To embrace this vision of children and to maximize the raw talents and abilities that reside in each and every child, I feel strongly that a leader must be guided by the following four beliefs:

1. *All* children can learn and must be given the opportunity to participate in high levels of social and intellectual engagement.
2. The dignity of children, as well as respect for their personal circumstances, family, culture, and linguistic diversity, must always be affirmed.
3. Children learn in their own way and at their own individual pace through the active participation and guidance of an adult.
4. Learning is a cognitive and social process, and play is an integral part of both dynamics.

Children achieve their full potential when adults are responsive to their strengths and needs throughout their early years. Additionally, in order for that potential to be fully realized, children must be provided with a rich array of daily experiences across multiple domains of learning that promote intellectual curiosity, awe and wonderment, imagination, spontaneity, communication, problem solving, and critical thinking.

Valuing Human Potential in Adults

The quality of human potential isn't limited to children. This is something that is too often forgotten in the field of education, where we spend the bulk of our energy on developing children's potential. Great leaders have to be able to recognize the potential in adults as well.

A few years ago, I was asked to transform the University Child Development Center at the University of the District of Columbia into a university lab school. It had to be more than just a child care facility. The provost was adamant that in order for the center to remain in the college of arts and sciences, it had to be a place where teachers could come for training, where psychology and nursing students could come and do observations, and where students could complete their student-teaching practicum requirements. The lab school was also required to provide opportunities for faculty members to conduct small-scale, field-initiated research.

Up to the challenge, I took over the preexisting program and reorganized it. To do that, I had to hire new staff. I believe that children need to see men in roles of responsive caregiving, and that was why we hired Mr. Jim as an assistant teacher.

There was something about him I picked up on during the hiring process. He wasn't fully trained in early childhood, but I saw something in him. Something I call *potential*. He showed a willingness to learn and an eagerness that reminded me of myself at that age. So we brought him on.

Mr. Jim had been through his own share of challenges. He was a single parent raising two children, a boy and a girl, by himself. He had recently lost his living accommodations due to back rent and was living with relatives. However, despite all of his challenges, he exhibited a "can-do" attitude and a desire to go to school to learn more about early childhood education.

Still, there were obstacles. We had some rough times. The fact of the matter was, in the beginning, he was just an okay employee. During his first year with us we ran into more than one situation that almost caused him to lose his job.

He was especially frustrating to the director of the place—a new leader herself who I was working with. She was incredibly bright, a crackerjack teacher, and it was easy to see why she and Mr. Jim didn't see eye to eye.

"I want him gone," she told me almost immediately.

And I could've said yes. I would have been within my rights. But I didn't.

"If I fire Jim for you," I reasoned, "you will never learn how to work with difficult staff. You have to look at what is beneath the surface with people."

She wasn't happy about it. But I wanted her to work through the issues with him. I wanted her to learn, as my mother taught me, to develop tolerance and understanding for people who come from different experiences and backgrounds. It went back to the root of human potential. What makes people tick? What was beneath the surface when it came to Mr. Jim? I wanted her to look for his underdeveloped talent—his human potential.

In the end, we kept him on, and we found out. Today Mr. Jim is one of our prized employees. His supervisor—that same director who wanted him out the door in the early days—will humbly admit as much. He has evolved not only in terms of additional duties and responsibilities acquired, but his growth as a classroom teacher has been inspiring. There is just something about Mr. Jim that children respond to.

Mr. Jim is just the sort of person I'm talking about when I say that opportunities are lost in this field by not having the willingness to understand people we don't immediately identify with. If we don't start with valuing the human condition, we lose out on the potential of high-performing staff.

People can exceed your expectations, but you have to nurture what's inside of them. Some say that all children are geniuses, and it's our responsibility to find the genius that lies within them and to bring it to the surface. The same thing is true with the human potential of adults. If you don't value adult human development, how can you be a developer of young children? After all, it is the adults you work with—or even hire and coach—who are teaching the children.

I tell people that I am a talent scout. As a leader in this field, I see it as part of my job description to seek out individuals who show a spark of potential to contribute in a profound way to making the educational experience better for children. Great leaders are always on the lookout for people with diverse skills and perspectives who will be able to contribute to their leadership agenda.

I once came across a veteran teacher who showed significant potential to become an outreach agent for our cause. When I floated the idea her way, she was receptive to it. Before long, I moved her out of her self-contained classroom and into outreach training. She became an exceptional demonstration teacher for the district. Afterward, she said, "Maurice saw something in me that I didn't see in myself."

This is part of our responsibility as leaders: to see in others what they do not yet see in themselves and to help them along the path to self-discovery.

Cultivating Human Potential

Ask yourself the following questions to begin—or improve—the process of recognizing and drawing out the human potential in others:

1. When in your professional or personal life has someone seen your potential? How did that feel? What was the result?
2. How do you create opportunities for children and adults to learn and grow?
3. When have you overlooked someone's potential because he or she was different from you? What happened? What will you do next time?
4. Next time you are frustrated with someone you supervise or a child you teach, stop and ask yourself, "What is this person's potential? What can I do to ensure that this person's potential is realized?"

Maximizing Human Potential

Always start from the assumption that all children and adults are gifted and talented, and that it is your job as a leader to find those gifts and talents and to unleash and activate them. In order for individuals around you to reach their full potential, you must be brave enough to set aside your biases and preconceived notions and search for the greatness that resides within the children and adults you work with. You must see beyond their present capabilities to a future state where they are effective and successful. Then you can create a strategy around how to maximize their potential, providing words of encouragement rather than discouragement and giving both children and adults the benefit of the doubt. Build on people's strengths and look for what they do well. When you seek and draw out human potential, you are doing the right thing not just for children but for everyone within your leadership circle of control.

Children and adults alike seek purpose and meaning in their endeavors. Therefore, in order to unleash their hidden talents and abilities, leaders must create environments that are arenas of opportunity for children and adults to explore, discover, and invent the genius that resides within them.

Knowledge

Perplexity is the beginning of knowledge.

Khalil Gibran

"This isn't going to be fun," the school director groaned under her breath.

We were on our way to meet with two of our assistant teachers who had just given a presentation to a group of parents. The presentation had been intended as an exploration for the parents regarding the roles of science, technology, engineering, and math (STEM) in the school. Unfortunately, the event had gotten a lukewarm reception to say the least. Both the director and I knew that this outcome didn't have to do with the program itself. Rather, it had to do with the presentation of the assistant teachers who had delivered it.

Both of the teachers in question were men, and both of them were known for having large egos. Neither one was the type to handle criticism well. The director was right: "fun" did not look to be on the schedule in the next hour.

"Let me try talking to them first," I told her. I had an idea. I wasn't sure that it would work. But it had to be worth a shot anyway.

The director was only too happy to oblige. "Be my guest," she invited.

A minute later we were sitting in her office around a table, facing both of the assistant teachers. I could tell by the guarded looks on their faces that they weren't expecting good news. Doubtless the traditional method of reading off a list of their faults would create the fireworks that the director was expecting. But traditional criticism wasn't the approach I decided to take that day.

I leaned forward in my chair, and folded my hands on the table. "Why don't we do this a little differently than usual?" I began. "Instead of us telling you what we thought about the exploration, you tell us what you thought about it.

What do you think went well, and where do you think there could have been improvement?"

The assistant teachers glanced at each other. For a moment that felt longer than it actually was, no one spoke. Finally, one of them cleared his throat.

"Honestly," he admitted, "I think we could have done better."

Then the director and I sat by and listened as the two of them delivered to themselves every piece of criticism we'd come up with. As they spoke, I marveled inwardly at the phenomenon that was taking place. The teachers were not just dealing with the issues of the presentation on a superficial level. They were going deeper than that, exploring their own strengths and weaknesses as educators. In a nutshell, through personal reflection, they were unearthing fundamental knowledge about themselves as human beings.

After the review was over and they had gone, the director turned to me. "That went much smoother than I thought it would," she said appreciatively. And it had.

What Is Knowledge?

My exercise with the assistant teachers that day stemmed from a personal core value of mine: that of inspiring knowledge in others. But what is knowledge? How does our understanding of it expand or change based on our work in the field of early childhood education? And how does it help us do the right thing for children?

In my view, a knowledgeable leader is not someone who is all knowing. Rather, he or she is someone who is all seeking. These individuals investigate. They ask questions. *How? What if? Why?* To be a successful leader in the field of early childhood education, you must be a seeker and a distributor of knowledge. And the seeking of knowledge is driven by one key element: curiosity.

Curiosity sounds simple, but the power in this one small concept knows no bounds. In curiosity we find the catalyst that has spurred the discovery and the growth of knowledge throughout all of human history. The children whose lives we seek to enrich are already in touch with this incredible learning tool. Anyone who has worked with young children knows that you cannot leave them in a room with a pile of blocks without witnessing curiosity manifest itself. At once, the questions come to life: *What designs can be pieced together out of these blocks? What structures can be made? How high can the blocks be stacked before they topple over?* Children's natural curiosity propels them to discover the answers to these questions. What started out as a pile of unremarkable blocks suddenly increases a hundredfold in value. Why? Because blocks on their own are just blocks. But blocks mixed with curiosity yield a far greater treasure: knowledge.

Leaders in early childhood education should take their cues from how children construct knowledge. Children are naturally curious about everything around them. They have theories and hypotheses that they are constantly testing through exploration and experimentation. For us, the blocks may look different, but we can learn much from the children's curiosity that can be brought into our own lives. Curiosity about the way we work and teach will lead to experimentation. Experimentation will lead to innovation, and innovation can lead to new and powerful discoveries.

There is an old saying, "Curiosity killed the cat," that suggests that too much investigation, experimentation, or seeking of new knowledge can be dangerous. However, the rejoinder to that phrase goes, "But satisfaction brought him back." If we open ourselves up to seeking the answers to complex questions—and if we use methods of inquiry including hypothesizing, researching, experimenting, and reflecting—we are well on the road to becoming knowledgeable leaders.

One challenge that leaders face is that many in education are set in their old ways. They are reluctant to give curiosity free reign, and their argument is that they want proof that the experiment is going to work before they actually run the experiment. You can see the catch-22 in this logic. There can be no breakthrough results without the experimentation. And, since we're focusing on creativity, preferably there will be more than one result! The key lies in granting these experiments permission to happen in the first place.

When we open our eyes and look around us, we can see that the curiosity-and-experiment-based model has proven itself to be invaluable in other fields. Technology is one example. Many technology companies give their associates both the resources and the permission to wander down new paths of innovation. The result has been astronomical leaps in technological advancements over the past few decades. Here, as with the children and their wooden blocks, the combination of curiosity and experimentation has led to wondrous amounts of new knowledge.

Although we as early childhood educators promote and encourage exploration and experimentation among the children we work with, we ourselves are often experimentation adverse. Thinking outside the box is not always our road most traveled. To an outsider, it might look as though we're freer than most other disciplines, but nothing could be further from the truth. The truth is that we are all guilty of getting caught in our own webs of complacency. We gravitate toward staying in our lockstep, top-down regiments, and we trap ourselves into thinking that there is only one way to do what we do.

Knowledge is not a passive ideal. It is not a lofty, academic concept. It is practical, it is hands-on, and it is accessible to anyone, of any age, who chooses to engage in the joy of discovery, the joy of personal and intellectual renewal, and the joy of understanding that knowledge is power. It is up to us to create an environment—for children and adults—where the pursuit of knowledge is encouraged, rewarded, and celebrated.

The Knowledge Economy

We live in a knowledge economy. People in our global society are constantly in search of knowledge, because knowledge is power. Experts are sought out in every field to promote advancement. Geopolitical barriers have crumbled, giving us international access to people and ideas that are turning impossibilities into possibilities that we never dreamed of before. The knowledge economy goes beyond our old ways of doing things. It seeks to apply new skills and discoveries to how things work in the world—all through the vehicle of expanding knowledge.

As educators, we have a key part to play in this ever-evolving global network of knowledge. It is our responsibility to ensure that the children in our care exit our programs with the skills, knowledge, and dispositions they need to be successful in school and in life. The responsibility for creating appropriate learning experiences that will enable them to do this lies in our hands.

The leader's role in the knowledge arena is not to establish a culture where everything goes. We should not be interested in knowledge for knowledge's sake. A successful leader understands that knowledge is a tool—one that, in our field, will enable us to further the aim of enriching the lives of young children.

Knowledge is exchangeable, knowledge is transportable, and knowledge is in demand. It is our responsibility as leaders in early childhood education to see that the seeds of knowledge gathering are planted early and watered well. To ensure that this takes place, we must familiarize ourselves with the core quality of knowledge on four levels: knowledge of self, knowledge of others, knowledge of craft, and knowledge of leadership.

Self-Knowledge

Years of coaching leaders have shown me the places where leaders run into trouble. In many cases, the real flaws in an individual's leadership are not in the superficial areas of methods and tactics. Rather, they arise from a lack of knowledge of self.

A leader who has not developed self-knowledge cannot perform his or her role effectively. The reason for this is simple. If you do not know who you are and what makes you tick, it's hard to know where you are going, let alone how to lead others toward achieving their personal bests. Every strong house is built upon a strong foundation. For a leader, that foundation comes down to possessing self-knowledge and clarity about your personal core values.

Cultivating an awareness of who you are and how you operate in multiple arenas is a critical piece in the puzzle of developing effective leadership. Self-knowledge is not just about what you know. It is also about understanding what you don't know. It is about knowledge of your strengths, your weaknesses, and your overall temperament. It is about looking in the mirror and confronting some truths that may be uncomfortable. It is the willingness to see yourself as others see you.

Ask yourself: *Who are you? Why are you here? What are you good at? What difference do you plan to make in this world? How do others see you? What is your leadership style? What do you believe in so strongly that you would be willing to fall on the sword for it?* These are the types of questions that you should use to outline and inform your ultimate aspirations as a leader in this field of work.

Only after you have engaged in the task of self-exploration can you begin to use your personal strengths and self-confidence to foster self-knowledge in others. My experiment in allowing the assistant teachers to reflect on and assess their presentation to the parents is an example of the rewards of this way of thinking. Because I myself was strongly in touch with my personal core value of inspiring others to seek self-knowledge, the events of that afternoon were able to take their due course. Had I been in a place of self-doubt, the concept of allowing those teachers to analyze and draw strength from their own doubts would likely never have occurred to me. This is the power of self-knowledge in action.

To have self-knowledge is to be filled with wonder, adventure, curiosity, and creativity. We must understand the importance of this concept if we are to be successful as leaders. Leaders who have a good and realistic sense of self will instill confidence in those they lead and inspire them to do their personal best for the organization and for the children and families that they serve.

Knowledge of Others

In addition to having self-knowledge, it is equally as important to have knowledge of the people you lead. A leader must engage in understanding the knowledge, skills, and temperaments of his or her staff members and then must use that knowledge to inspire and maximize performance. This can be done through informal assessments such as casual observations, inventories such as multiple intelligences questionnaires, learning style assessments, or more formalized assessment tools such as the Myers-Briggs Type Indicator. Whatever method you use, it is important to develop a way of knowing your followers so you can adjust your leadership approach based on what you know about each person.

This does not mean that you are constantly changing your style to suit the idiosyncrasies of each individual; however, it does acknowledge that you know that adults, just like children, are not all the same and that one's leadership style does not fit all. For example, because I am very familiar with the Myers-Briggs assessment, I can fairly quickly and accurately figure out a person's personality type and manage them according to their style and temperament. However, the best way to gain knowledge of others is by wandering around listening and observing. That means that you need to come out of your office and go into classrooms as a matter of daily practice. Talk to the children and observe firsthand what the challenges are that the staff face. Then, when you talk to the teachers about their teaching practices you will be talking from a more authentic perspective.

Other ways of increasing your knowledge of others is through informal one on ones, where you get to learn things about the person's hopes, dreams, and aspirations. *How do they prefer to do their work? How do they prefer to receive feedback and general communication? How do they like to be recognized and rewarded? What you can do to make their job more doable?*

The bottom line is that just like children, adults also want to be seen, heard, valued, and respected.

Knowledge of Craft

In Japan, there is something called the lesson study. The lesson study is a process in which a teacher designs a lesson plan and then teaches the lesson in front of a group of other teachers. These teachers then give the presenting teacher feedback on the lesson. This process is as straightforward as they come, yet it is revered in Japanese culture for one simple reason: it works.

The Japanese lesson study is an example of craft knowledge at its best. Through its easy exchange of ideas, the lesson study gives knowledge the forum it needs to build on itself—and thrive. People come from all over the world to learn how to do it. As leaders in early education, this is the kind of group cooperation and knowledge exchange that is so important for us to promote the knowledge of our craft.

Craft knowledge, or "wisdom of craft," is the wealth of teaching knowledge that very skilled practitioners know and understand about their own practice. It is also the knowledge base about teaching and learning that effective leaders must have in order to lead an early learning community. The people that you lead must know that you know what you are talking about and that your knowledge base comes from a rich body of experience, research, and practice.

Early in the movement toward state content standards, teacher educators would often say about teachers' lack of craft knowledge, "You can't teach that which you do not know." Well, the same holds true for leaders: you can't lead on that which you have not experienced. It is important that leaders have experiential knowledge as well as theoretical knowledge about teaching young children. We must know and understand how to translate the principles of child development into a developmentally appropriate pedagogy of child development.

Similar to the Japanese lesson study, effective leaders must acquire the knowledge and skills they need to establish and maintain a community of professional practice—one that is committed to a process of continual inquiry, reflection, experimentation, and research in order to improve the craft of teaching.

Knowledge of Leadership

Effective leaders are always in search of new opportunities to sharpen their mental saws and deepen their understanding of the art and science of leadership. They achieve this through the acquisition of new skills, new knowledge, and new perspectives. Leaders who continue to expand their repertoire of skills throughout their careers are more likely to be successful. Too often, leaders are so consumed with the development of others that they forget that they have an obligation to themselves, and to those they lead, to continue to grow, stretch, and evolve as leaders.

Therefore, it is critical that leaders tend to their professional growth and development by continuing to enhance and refine their repertoire of leadership skills and knowledge throughout their professional careers. It all begins with the leader's personalized professional growth plan (PPGP). Your PPGP is your road map for where you are going and how you plan to get there. Use it to take stock of what you already know about leadership and which aspects of leadership you desire to know more about. Ask yourself: *What are your strengths, and how can you play to them? What are some developmental experiences that you could assign to yourself to gain new knowledge? Where are the arenas of opportunity, within your own bailiwick, in which you can stretch and grow as a leader, and learn something new?*

A great deal of leadership development comes as a result of reflection on everyday occurrences. Reflection is part of the knowledge-seeking journey. When you take the time to stop and reflect, new insights may be revealed for old problems. The new insights can draw new learning from those past experiences, and you will be able to apply the new knowledge to experiences in the future.

Leaders should seek new challenges inside and outside their organizations that will allow them to build on their current leadership skill set. For example, perhaps you want to try your hand at applying the situational leadership framework to an individual or a group. Or maybe you want to know more about creating professional learning communities. Regardless of your learning goals, you must have a platform for yourself that is built around a certain set of thoughtful questions: *What do you already know, and what are you already able to do as a leader? What do you want to know more about? How, and in what settings, do you want to learn? What internal and external developmental assignments will help you learn more about leadership? How will you measure your success at becoming more knowledgeable about leadership? How will you use the knowledge you seek to do the right thing for children?*

Knowledge at the Organizational Level

As on the level of self-knowledge, a leader at the organizational level embodies knowledge not by being all knowing but by being all seeking. If I think I have all the answers to all the questions, it's going to get me into trouble. But if I'm constantly seeking knowledge myself, then the rest of my organization will pick up on that. I would never ask you to do anything that I wouldn't do myself, and seeking knowledge is one of those things. In this way, I open the door for others to seek out knowledge as well.

Cultivating knowledge at the organizational level is largely environmental. As leaders, it falls to us to create an environment that supports creativity and experimentation. We do this by returning to the core quality of self-knowledge and modeling those traits ourselves. Ask yourself: *Do you model curiosity? Are you open to new information, or are you closed to it? Do you push other people to be curious about what is going on?* The mantra here is not, "I know." Rather, it becomes, "I wonder if that is possible."

What if we mixed three-year-olds, four-year-olds, and five-year-olds into a single class instead of organizing those three ages into separate classes? What would happen? You have to be willing to find out. By opening up and actively listening to others, you enable the transfer of knowledge to take place. Ideas spring from these dialogues that may be nothing like what you were expecting. That's the beauty and the utility of this process. You listen to people, and people listen to you.

Another facet of knowledge at the organizational level is being willing to step aside and give others the opportunity to manage the knowledge at times. In teaching, there is the saying "The sage on the stage, the guide on the side." It means that the one in the spotlight is supported by someone who is not in the spotlight. The same rule applies to leadership. Allowing others to take the stage fosters self-confidence and strengthens the organization as a whole.

This is the root of the culture that we as leaders in early education must seek to create. We want to construct the opportunities for people to collaboratively seek knowledge. We want to share the stage of knowledge. Most of all, we want to build a context of continual inquiry and reflection in our organizations. How can we accomplish these things? By returning to that same fundamental truth at the root of all knowledge: curiosity.

As leaders, we must set the standard for collaborative knowledge building by sharing the discoveries that our personal curiosity helps us unearth. When we share knowledge and curiosity with the adults we lead, those adults will in turn share those same things with the children in their care. For instance, say I am working on a citywide infant-toddler quality-improvement initiative. I come across a great article about infant-toddler curriculum. Rather than keep that article to myself, I'm going to send it out to everyone I work with. Actions like that start the exchange of ideas and discourse. The day that someone comes up to you and says, "I saw an article myself that I thought you might be interested in. Is it okay if I share it with the rest of the staff?" is when you know that you've set and reinforced the right example and that you have created the conditions in your organization that will allow knowledge building to flourish.

Once again, we are not interested in knowledge just for knowledge's sake. We should be interested in knowledge that leads to observable, proactive thinking and action. I have often participated in knowledge-building brainstorming sessions where the facilitator says, "In this room there are no bad ideas." Well, that is not exactly true. There are bad ideas. However, even bad ideas, in a knowledge-building organization, can lead to good ideas. I believe that you can teach people to think critically and to assess the essence of the bad idea and its implications for your desired outcomes. This can be fostered by engaging in a dialogue that asks the following questions: *How does this idea square with our vision and goals? What is good about this idea? How could we make it better? How could this idea in combination with other ideas have an impact on our organization?*

To make this equation function at the organizational level, it is imperative to set up clear standards of practice. Your standards of practice are more or less the ground rules. They define basic responsibilities: *What does the leader do? What do the teachers do? What do the parents do? What do the children do?* Every other organization in different arenas—medical, law, finance—has standards of practice. Education, meanwhile, has been slow to pick up on this incredibly useful tool. As leaders, it is time we changed that.

Standards of practice do not have to be limiting. They can and should be the framework within which curiosity and creativity are given free reign to bloom. For example, say I look at my institution's standards of practice, and I decide that this year we as a team are going to focus on decision making and communication. There is my framework. Within it, there are any number of domains: leading, teaching, learning, interacting with parents, facilitating community engagement, and so forth.

With this understanding in hand, I now have a platform to stand on. I can then go to the director of our school, who I supervise, and say, "You know the big picture. Now, within that, choose any one of these domains that you yourself are particularly interested in and work toward accomplishing that piece of the goal. Develop your own personal plan for it. I will see to it that you have the resources you need to pursue your knowledge seeking in this area." The director has no hard-and-fast rules for how she should go about pursuing her goal, and that gives her the freedom to follow her curiosity and to experiment. However, I, as the leader of the organization, know that at the end of the day, what she is working toward will benefit the institution as a whole. This gives me the accountability I need to continue to promote the growth and exchange of knowledge.

Let me give you an example of this theory in action. Recently at the lab school, we have been experimenting with ways to create space where children can explore science, technology, engineering, and math on their own terms. To accomplish this, a shift at the organizational level took place: we changed the plan of adults defining how children will use the space to the new plan of the children themselves defining how they will use it.

Our decision to conduct this experiment was an example of our culture of continual inquiry and reflection. Nevertheless, it perplexed some of the teachers. One in particular had serious doubts about it. He was convinced that the children would not be able to do work that was constructive and meaningful in the space without adult guidance and direction. So, without telling anybody what he was up to, he took the initiative and launched his own inquiry. The question he posed was this: if we turned the space and the direction over to the children, would they be able to come up with ways of using it that were as good as the ideas that we adults had?

This teacher really didn't think so, and he set out to prove it. For his personal experiment, he put some recycled materials out on a table in the afternoon to see what, if anything, the children would do with them. Then he documented his observations.

What he found was that without any guidance at all, the children took those recycled materials and started building things with them. And that wasn't the end of it. Before long, some other children began taking the materials up to the elevated area in the room's loft and dropping them off the top of it. The teacher noted with interest that, in order to keep this game going, the children came up with a strategy among themselves regarding how they were going to get those fallen materials back up to the loft again so that they could continue dropping them. The sense of cooperation that they created deeply impressed him. He concluded that without adult direction, the children had used the materials he provided to manifest creativity in terms of construction and to foster cooperation with one another to get something done. In this way, a point was proven that expanded the knowledge of our organization.

This teacher's experiment could not have happened without the right knowledge-seeking framework in place. The environment in which he lives and works made it permissible for him to investigate his questions regarding the natural skill and disposition of young children and to answer those questions not only for himself but for everyone else on the staff as well.

As leaders and promoters of knowledge-seeking environments, we must strive to create spaces and places in the field where people can experiment, make mistakes, and re-create experiments. People need to know that it is safe for them to examine new ideas and theories and to try out new things. And they need to know that if those things don't work, they can always go back and figure out how to make them better. As long as this takes place within strong standards of practice, the result will always be expanded knowledge, and the organizations we lead can only become stronger.

Knowledge at the Classroom Level

During my debriefing with the two assistant teachers who gave that subpar presentation, I asked them a question. "What would you have said to a parent who had asked you, 'Why should our children bother with things like science, technology, engineering, and math (STEM)? They are only three to five years old. Why aren't you focusing on literacy, or why can't they just play?'"

The teachers thought about this for a moment. Then one of them replied, "I would have said that we teach them these things because children are natural scientists. They are full of questions; they are full of awe and wonderment. Furthermore, we can teach them literacy through STEM, and they can be playful at the same time."

It was an answer that would have satisfied any parent, and he was right. That assistant teacher had been paying close attention to the way children worked at the classroom level. Because of that, he had knowledge of the children that he was teaching.

Leadership at the classroom level revolves around this student-teacher connection. It is imperative that we encourage teachers to have knowledge of the children they are teaching: their abilities, their dispositions, and their political, social, and economic contexts. Only then will teachers be able to respond to situations with an appropriate leadership style themselves, using their diverse range of strategies and protocols to achieve the best possible effect for the children in their care.

As with any form of knowledge, the seed of this student-teacher connection is curiosity. Teachers must always be curious about the children they teach, and they must apply critical thinking to that curiosity. Why does Heather have trouble interacting with others? How can we help her become more socially competent? What can we do to make children's portfolios more engaging? This in-depth engagement is the root of the bond that will strengthen the core quality of knowledge at the classroom level.

But knowledge at the classroom level doesn't stop with children. It includes their families as well. Parents and other family members are integral to early childhood education, and as such it is important to include them in our work. At our lab school, we have created an environment that lets parents know that they are at the center of our work. When I bring a guest through the school, it isn't the children's work that is prominently displayed in the main corridor; it's the work of the parents—they participate in family events at the school where they learn and create in much the same way that the children do and their work is displayed prominently in the entrance and other community spaces. In this way, we communicate to parents that they are a part of our knowledge-building organization, that they are welcome here, and that they are an integral part of their children's education. They, as much as us, are part of the culture of curiosity and discovering new solutions, and their contributions have a significant role to play in the role of knowledge at the classroom level.

Perhaps the best part of the core quality of knowledge is that it begins with self-knowledge, and once you have traveled down the tiers to organizational and classroom-level knowledge, it leads right back to self-knowledge again. I witnessed this firsthand during one of my recent visits to the lab school. Everyone was gathered in the art studio, and there was a wonderful hum in the room. All of the children, perhaps thirty in all, were on task. The positive art and language activity was enough to make anyone's heart swell with joy. Then, two four-year-old girls, Maya and Jeanette, had a new idea.

"Want to play hide-and-seek?" Jeanette asked.

"Yes," agreed Maya.

So Jeanette scurried off to hide. Maya began counting, "One . . . two . . ." Plenty of adults were in the room, and they were engaged with the other children. But these two little girls decided that art wasn't for them right at that moment, and they struck up their own course of action. They knew that they didn't have to go with the crowd, and that it was safe to think for themselves. Thinking for themselves led to thinking outside the box.

I took great pride in the understanding that the environment that we had created for these little girls through our own shared core quality of knowledge had come full circle and was enabling the children in our care to begin to develop self-knowledge and self-actualization on their own.

Cultivating Knowledge

To proactively cultivate knowledge in yourself and others, consider the following questions. Answer them for each type of knowledge: self-knowledge, knowledge of others, knowledge of craft, and leadership knowledge.

1. What are the multiple sources from which you acquire knowledge?
2. How do you distribute knowledge to others?
3. How do or can you make knowledge central to your leadership practice?
4. How can you use technology to access and manage knowledge?

Expanding Knowledge

On one end of the spectrum, the leadership quality of knowledge is about creativity and staying open to the possibilities of the imagination. It is about keeping a line of communication open with that fundamental part of ourselves that finds fascination and wonder in the world. On the other end of that same spectrum, knowledge is also analytical and logical. It is informed by discipline and by high-standards practice. When these two aspects of knowledge come together and find balance, the benefits that we can achieve through this leadership quality are limitless.

To be an authentic leader, you need to be curious and to take calculated risks about the things you don't yet know. It's important for you to keep the dialogue of knowledge open. If a teacher or a child asks you a question that you don't know the answer to, you don't make something up to save face. You don't shrug your shoulders and walk away. You say, "I don't know, but let's figure it out and see what we can do together to fix the problem." As a leader, you must develop the habit of mind that seeks to understand the dynamic of what is going on around you. This above all else will help you to create the knowledge-based culture that is the foundation for successful leadership in early childhood education. This leadership will in turn ultimately help you do the right thing for the children themselves.

Social Justice

Great teaching is about so much more than education;
it is a daily fight for social justice.

Arne Duncan

I have always had a disposition toward social justice. Even as a child, I had an incredibly strong sense about good and bad, right and wrong, fairness and unfairness, and empathy for others. I loved cheering for the underdog. Of course, as a child I did not have a name for this sense of justice. It was simply about doing unto others as you would have them do unto you—I learned that at home from my parents. As I matured and became clearer about my perspective regarding the human condition, the easy notion of doing unto others as you would have them do unto you became more nuanced.

I grew up during the civil rights movement of the late 1950s and early 1960s. In those days, it was not unusual for the original Freedom Singers to present concerts in my community in their efforts to educate the public about the struggle for civil rights in the South and to raise funds for their cause. Their presence brought to the fore the blatant injustices in my own upstate New York community as well as what was happening in the South. Between what I was experiencing in my daily personal life and what I was observing of the civil rights struggle via television and newspaper accounts, I now had a name for what I was experiencing and observing—social injustice.

I am sure that during that period of time I developed a beginning level of consciousness regarding fairness and equity that continues as a central part of me to this day. Of course, these early experiences have been supplemented by my studies of the social sciences, my reading of historical injustices, and my own experiences as an education social activist. Today, my understanding of social justice is about doing the right thing for *all* people, which often means taking a critical stance against injustice and inequality across a broad spectrum of social and political issues. Taken together, these experiences have formed my belief that leadership for social justice must be integral to the mission, vision, and passion of an exemplary, transformational leader.

Promoting Social Justice

My core value of social justice springs from being consciously aware and willing to surface issues and take action on behalf of individuals and groups that have been historically marginalized due to race, color, gender, sexual orientation, ethnicity, language, culture, or disability. Therefore, social justice is strongly rooted in my desire and my perceived obligation to make our society a better place—social justice is a driving force behind my leadership agenda.

To promote social justice is to have a strong inclination not to stand quietly when someone is being treated unfairly. As a child, I often stepped in to help another child who was getting bullied, even at personal risk to myself. Now, as a leader in the field of early childhood education, I often step in when I feel that a child is being bullied or mistreated due to bad public policy, a biased perception of his or her race, class, language, or culture, or unfair instructional practices that place a child at a decided disadvantage. Exemplary leaders are required to point out injustices wherever they see them and often find themselves in the unenviable position of having to ask the question: *Is this situation right, fair, and equitable?*

I remember early in my leadership journey, while directing the Tufts University Educational Day Care Center, I encountered one of my first of what would be many social-justice leadership challenges. The center had been established during a period when many colleges and universities were responding to the demands of students and faculty to become more socially responsive. Students and faculty at Tufts wanted and needed child care. It turned out, understandably so, that most of the students who used the center were income eligible for subsidies from the state. Plus, all of the faculty and staff paid tuition on a sliding-fee scale. This combination of limited-funding streams was hardly enough to meet the budgetary requirements of running the center; I had been charged by the dean of the College of Arts and Sciences to make the center financially self-sufficient.

It came to my attention through some of my child care colleagues in the Medford-Somerville area that the state was going to release a request for proposals (RFP) on child care support and that it might be to my center's economic advantage to have a contract with the state and thus have a steady and reliable source of income. This appeared to me as a viable solution to the challenge of making the center financially self-sufficient. There were plenty of children in the catchment area who met the low-income requirements of the state, and we could arrange bus transportation to transport the children to the center and from the Mystic Public Housing Development.

I must admit I was not at all prepared for the push back that I received from the parents who were receiving subsidies for their child care. They, and the parents paying tuition, did not want "that element" from the housing project at the center. Up until that point my advocacy for children had been limited to African American urban children from underresourced communities. Now I was confronted with bias against white children from an underresourced community. The debate went on for several weeks. However, my philosophical and political stance and my economic arguments finally prevailed. It was at that point that I realized that my advocacy for social justice was directed toward *all* children, and it has remained that way throughout my professional career.

The NAEYC code of ethical conduct is very clear in its principle regarding our responsibilities to children: "Above all, we shall not harm children. We shall not participate in practices that are emotionally damaging, physically harmful, disrespectful, degrading, dangerous, exploitative, or intimidating to children." This is a credo that should be embraced by all who seek to work on behalf of young children, and it should serve as a guidepost for exemplary leaders.

The Early Education Achievement Gap

There is one very clear, straightforward reason why social justice is critical to the field of early education. That reason is called "the early education achievement gap."

The early education achievement gap is most clearly defined by the Hart-Risley study of 1995. In this study, two researchers—Betty Hart and Todd Risley—examined the vocabulary development of children from three different economic walks of life: poor welfare families, working-class families, and professional families. Hart and Risley followed the children from ten months to age three, listening to, counting, and recording the words that were spoken in those different family environments.

What they discovered sent shock waves ricocheting through the educational community. Whereas a child in a low-income family heard only 616 words per hour on average, a child in a college-educated family was exposed to 2,153 words in the same stretch of time. Hart and Risley termed this difference the "thirty-million-word gap," because children from college-educated families had heard approximately 30 million more words than children from low-income families by the time they were three years old.

The effects of this gap are clearly documented in education. By the time they are nine or ten, the same children who had been exposed to strong vocabularies by the age of three are earning strong scores on vocabulary and syntax tests. The same cannot be said for their low-income peers, and the gap between the high and low scores is not a narrow one. In view of these facts, we can make only one conclusion: the achievement gap begins very early in life, and it is an injustice that children from underresourced communities suffer simply because of where they have been born.

Another jolting piece of research is Walter Gilliam's 2005 Yale University study, "Prekindergarteners Left Behind." After completing his research on state prekindergarten expulsion rates, Gilliam concluded the expulsion rates of prekindergarten children (ages three and four) in state-supported prekindergarten programs were triple the national rate of expulsion of children in public K–12 schools in the same forty states. More disturbingly, boys were expelled 4.5 times as frequently as girls, and African American children were twice as likely to be expelled as Latinos or Caucasians. Bob Moses, the founder of the nationally recognized Algebra Project, has coined the term *sharecropper education* to refer to the very low expectations placed on black children in schools. The term also describes the inadequacy and inequality of the current system of education for children from underresourced communities.

We in leadership positions have the power to change these unjust realities. Some of us argue that the responsibility of addressing the achievement gap falls on the shoulders of parents alone. Some of us see the prekindergarten expulsion rate as a parental, state, or cultural problem. Still others view the issue as a "that's just the way it is" kind of problem. But I am not willing to stand on the sidelines twiddling my thumbs, waiting for the world to become perfect. As leaders and educators in this field, we are once again faced with the question of our circle of concern versus our circle of control. Is it realistic for us to eliminate all social injustice in our society single-handedly? No. However, we are not powerless to effect change.

We have the ability—and the responsibility—to do the right thing for children by ensuring that we use every minute of the day that they are in our care to its fullest potential. In this way, we do our part to address social justice and to make the greatest possible difference in children's lives.

Leadership and Social Justice

A leader in the field of early childhood education is an agent for change. When viewed through the lens of social justice, the goal of what we seek to change defines itself more clearly, and it is this: we as leaders are trying to change the circumstances under which people—children and adults alike—operate in our educational system and in society as a whole.

Education has the potential to be the great equalizer. It can remove barriers, sweep away preexisting notions of limitation, and elevate children to a place where they are able to build successful lives for themselves in the world. Education itself is a change agent in that it empowers young children to take control of their lives. When used to its full potential, education has the power to blunt out the injustice that arises from social and economic circumstances.

As leaders, our responsibility is to make sure that education for every child, and especially for those from underresourced communities, lives up to this potential. To do this, our sense of social justice must be absolute and unwavering. It is our task to define and to uphold the pillars of right and wrong. Above all else, we must disentangle ourselves from the political webs complicating the field of education and remain focused on our true goal: bettering the lives of the children themselves.

While serving as a consultant to a public charter school in Washington DC, I noticed a sign on the door of a pre-K classroom that stated children who had not brought in money for the field trip to the pumpkin patch were to report to another room for the day. I was outraged. Beyond the fact that I saw no intellectual or academic reason for the children to go on such a trip, I was bothered by the humiliation and alienation that the children would experience as a result of their parent forgetting to send the money or not being able to afford the fees.

I went immediately to the principal's office and expressed my displeasure. I described the inequity in the situation: a public school denying children the opportunity to participate in school experiences due to a child's lack of resources would marginalize his or her membership in the community of learners. Surprisingly, and equally as scary, the principal knew nothing about the practice of charging fees and that practice was subsequently discontinued. Had I remained silent, and/or viewed this injustice on a gray scale, the policy of exclusion would have probably continued, and many children would have been harmed by such a practice.

To exemplify social justice as a leader is to always be clear and focused on your intentions. To do this well requires what I like to term the three Vs: vision, voice, and visibility. You need vision to see the injustices around you, voice to bring them to the forefront, and the visibility to correct them. Leaders with the three Vs have a working knowledge of the social and political context of their environment and a strategic plan to apply the knowledge to the injustice they are trying to address, and they are able to exercise the required level of political acumen necessary to remedy the situation.

Too many would-be leaders are content to stand on the sidelines, wringing their hands and wishing things were different. These men and women fail to understand that those who stand idly by and allow injustice to happen are just as guilty as those who are responsible for the injustice in the first place. As leaders with a strong sense of social justice, however, we are not wishers. We are doers. By devoting our energy to the three Vs, we push ourselves toward actively making an impact in the field of education. We put ourselves in motion to ensure that there is a level playing field in education for all children, from all walks of life. We do this by creating programs that are robust, challenging, and intellectually stimulating. We do it by inspiring children to rise to their full personal potential. We are the change agents that can make high-quality educational programs for young children from all walks of life happen. In this way, we do our part to fight injustice.

Social Justice at the Individual Level

As with any core value, social justice begins at the individual level. Before we can make decisions about what is right and wrong for children, we must have a clear understanding of what is right and wrong for ourselves. An action made from sound logic will turn a ship in the right direction. But an action made from a place of personal conviction will move the ship to its destination with many times more power and speed.

Developing a strong individual sense of social justice requires awareness of yourself, your immediate environment, and of those things happening in the larger society. The challenge here lies in the fact that today's society is fond of talking about things in shades of gray. However, some things are absolute and irrefutable. For example, many children in this country, through no fault of their own but rather through where they fall in the social, political, and economic birth lottery, are subjected to a continual cycle of inadequate support and services, including low-quality early childhood programs, and consequently get off to an uneven start that likely remains persistent throughout their lives.

How do you define *right*, exactly? What, really, is bad or wrong? These are lines that every leader must draw for him or herself. The question is how to draw them. For me, drawing the line as it relates to young children is fairly simple. I just tell people to ask themselves the following question: *Would you want your child or grandchild to be in this situation?* In most cases, I find that the shades of gray tend to disappear pretty quickly when looked at in this context. If the answer is no—it's not good enough for your child or any child you love—then it's not good enough for anyone's child. That is the end of the story. That is a stand for social justice.

As leaders, we must always be in touch with our personal moral compass of right and wrong, fair and unfair, because that is the foundation from which all of our decisions spring. By remaining vigilantly attuned to this compass, we can act in a way that keeps the ship of education pointed due north and cutting swiftly along in the right direction.

Social Justice at the Organizational Level

Social justice at the organizational level returns to the concept that education can and should be the great equalizer. Education can close some of the opportunity and resource gaps that many children experience from birth. However, this will only happen when leaders in our field take off their rose-tinted glasses and acknowledge that for many children, and adults, life is not fair—people are marginalized, sorted, and selected out of the abundant opportunities that exist in this country. Next, having recognized the problem, leaders must become relentless in their efforts to do something about solving the problem.

To achieve this goal, we must work at two levels. The first is within our organizations themselves, and the second is on the level of public policy on behalf of our organizations.

Here's what this can look like at the organizational level: The Early Childhood Leadership Institute is an organization that I founded over fifteen years ago. It has as one of its primary goals the recruitment and development of men and Latinos, two underrepresented groups in the field of early childhood education. This seemingly simple goal shines a light on the organization's commitment to creating a workforce that is reflective of two historically underrepresented groups in our field.

Leaders have the responsibility to ensure that strong programs and practices that promote social justice are in place in their organizations. Think again of the thirty-million-word gap for a moment. It is a known fact that children from underresourced communities are not read to at home as frequently as is optimal. This is due in large part to the social and economic injustices that their families and communities often experience. To correct this social injustice, our lab school has implemented a program that guarantees that the children in our care are read to at least twice every day that they are with us. Additionally, we have created a lending library that provides the children and their families with access to high-quality books.

We do not take the position that providing these opportunities for learning is solely the responsibility of the parents. To the contrary, we see it as our collective responsibility to respond to inequality by providing the supports that begin to mediate the lack of resources of children and families who are at a disadvantage. In this way, we exercise social justice within our circle of control, and we play our part in doing the right thing for children. Reading to children and creating a lending library are simple—and impactful—ways that all early childhood educators can help close the word gap.

Equalizing the playing field within individual educational institutions is a key element to achieving social justice in education. But it is not the only goal that we as leaders must set our sights on. On a larger scale, our task is to influence the public policies that affect these institutions.

Our circle of control in this arena often extends further than we typically imagine. As leaders in this field, we have the power and the authority to push for public policy that ensures universal high-quality pre-K programs. One social-justice issue we should push onto the political stage right now is compensation for those who work in education. Although we claim as a society that education is of important value to us, we do not pay teachers very much, and we pay early childhood teachers even less. The unfortunate fact of the matter is that teaching as a profession has become one of the last vestiges of worker exploitation. The early childhood industry has been built on the backs of mostly women who have been consigned to low-wage, low-status jobs in child care while shouldering the responsibility to care for and educate the next generation of intellects, workers, and leaders. This is inherently unjust and it must be addressed.

As the men and women who work with these teachers on a daily basis, we are the ones with front-row seats to the effects that low wages have on the education system. We are the ones who hold the proof that quality training for these individuals makes a difference in the results of their work with children. We are the ones whose voices carry the weight in this field, and as such we must use those voices to create the change we wish to see in the education landscape.

Social Justice at the Classroom Level

All teaching occurs within a socio-political-cultural context. In classrooms, where social justice sits at the core of the teaching-learning process, teachers are conscious of their biases and prejudices around historically marginalized groups. With this awareness comes the responsibility to confront these perceptions and work through how these socio-culturally constructed perceptions influence and inform how they interact with the children in their care and the families that they serve. This is not easy and it takes courage. Those who have taught know that at some point in their career they have developed positive and negative biases toward specific children. That is to be expected. We are only human, after all. But it is the teacher with a strong sense of social justice who recognizes that bias for what it is, where it is coming from, and how to remove it from their verbal and nonverbal interactions with children. Children have strong bias detectors—they know when they are treated differently, even if they may not be able to articulate the experience as social injustice. Teachers who are able to eliminate bias from their interactions with children understand that it makes them more whole and effective as teachers.

Leaders who support teachers of young children must serve as a constant reminder and chronicler of the values and vision that support social justice in all aspects of the organization, including the classroom. They must develop as heightened a bias detector as the children and be willing to engage in the sometimes difficult conversations with teachers about observed teacher behaviors, classroom dialogue, and pedagogical practices that on their face seem unfair and in practice tend to marginalize individuals or groups of children. Leaders should provide a pathway for teachers to understand and develop a stance for social justice. There are many ways to do this, including:

- providing formal professional development opportunities;
- taking part in authentic conversations with staff regarding biases, fairness, and unfairness;
- reading and discussing accounts of historical struggles for justice;
- doing self-work that confronts previously held assumptions regarding fairness and justice; and
- pursuing an antibias curriculum.

In addition to the self-work that is required to become an effective teacher of social justice, it is also necessary to delve into the historical and current struggles of traditionally marginalized groups. It is important to seek to understand how you will create a community of learners within your classroom who are attuned to issues of empathy, caring, fairness, social responsibility, and inclusion. From day one, the environment should send out these messages from what is said and from what is seen throughout the classroom. The teacher should always be attuned to random acts of injustice no matter how insignificant they might appear on the surface.

On a recent visit to the lab school, I walked into the classroom to find Kristina eating a snack. This in itself would not have been remarkable, except that when I glanced at the clock, I saw that it was about a half hour before the scheduled snacktime. Moreover, a few other children without snacks were loitering around, and Kristina had a touch of smugness on her face as she nibbled away at her apple.

Right away, I pulled the teacher aside. "Why is Kristina having her snack early?" I asked.

"Well, she was hungry," replied the teacher. There was a ray of defensiveness in his tone. He knew that I had a reason for asking.

"But snacktime isn't for another half hour," I pressed.

"I know, but she has food issues, so I really think we should just feed her when she asks for it."

Before I knew it, the whole long story about Kristina's unique situation was flooding my eardrums. No detail was spared in the telling. I took a breath and waited for the teacher to finish. Then I said, "I understand what you're saying. All the same, it's an injustice to the other children to see that she gets to eat while the rest of them have to wait until snacktime. In the future, if you want to put all of the snacks out so that any of the children can take them whenever they want, that could be a solution. But we have to be careful not to send the message to the other children that Kristina is privileged."

My response to the situation with Kristina was based on my core value regarding social justice at the classroom level. Social justice is born of our notions of fairness, equality, and recognition. These things need to apply at the classroom level as much as they do at the personal and organizational levels if we are to reform the education system into the equalizer that it needs to be in our society.

As a leader, I always encourage my teachers to remain highly attuned to the quality of social justice. I do this by calling attention to the methods they use to implement social justice in the classroom. Do you know that child is a second-language learner? I might ask. Or, did you see that child had her hand up, but you passed over her and went to the other children instead? I encourage them to use their classroom knowledge to do the right thing for children by promoting social justice.

Our behavior at the classroom level is the most direct tool we have when it comes to instilling the quality of social justice in the children we teach. Nowhere does this have a greater impact than on students from underresourced communities. Often, children from these communities come to us as geniuses. They are at-promise children on par with peers from better-resourced communities. Then, it is the teacher's poor attitude, low expectations, and indifference toward helping them reach their full potential that often places them "at risk" of not being successful in school and in life. Closing the achievement gap is an issue of social justice. Our actions matter. When we teach in classrooms that are not caring communities of learners, where there is an absence of engaging, robust, challenging learning, we are in fact practicing what Martin Haberman calls "the pedagogy of poverty." As leaders we cannot afford to let these injustices slide. We must convey to all children in our care that in our classrooms they are known, valued, unique, emotionally safe, and brilliant. By staying vigilant and keeping our eyes and ears open, we as leaders can promote social justice in the classroom. Through our day-to-day actions, we must do everything in our power to help teachers we supervise and children in our care to understand the basic principles of justice and equity. In this way, we are doing more than strengthening the foundation of education. We are instilling in our children a core value that they will then be able to carry forth with them into the world, where they can use it to make a difference of their own.

Cultivating Social Justice

You may begin—or continue—to actively cultivate social justice in yourself and others by reflecting on and discussing the following questions:

1. Are you willing to speak up for policies and practices that you feel are unjust? If there are times when you want to, but are afraid, what is holding you back? What can you do to gain the courage to speak up?
2. In what ways do you keep social justice at the center of your vision and practice?
3. Have you examined your own personal biases, their origins, and how they influence your leadership style?
4. How do you engage children in authentic conversations regarding issues of social justice?
5. What strategies can you use to advance social justice?

The Core of Social Justice

Whether at the individual, the organizational, or the classroom level, the leadership quality of social justice does not allow for shades of gray. It pretty much defines who you are as a human being and what it means to be human. Transformational leadership requires the leader to stand for what is right and just. Social-justice leadership requires the leader to pursue issues of fairness and equity as his or her personal strategy for doing the right thing for children.

You must identify the fibers of your own moral fabric in no uncertain terms. When you do this, you empower yourself to act from more than just sound logic. You empower yourself to act from the heart. From this position of strong moral ground, and as a leader, you can do the right thing for children by promoting and exemplifying social justice in early childhood education to the maximum benefit of all.

Competence

Competence as a leader is having all the tools for what ever the occasion and knowing when to use what tool. It's ignoring the path of least resistance and doing what is best for everyone involved.

Russell White

What is the difference between knowledge and competence? Simply put, knowledge is the sum of your understanding and information about your field of endeavor. It is the result of education, training, research, readings, and conversations with peers and experts. Competence, by contrast, is about what you do with your knowledge. It is knowledge put into actionable behaviors that become a part of your leadership practice.

Research and information are valuable things. However, as leaders in this field, we are only as powerful as our ability to use them in practical ways to orchestrate positive educational outcomes for children. We are not learning for learning's sake alone. We are learning with the purpose of bettering the lives of the children in our care. We are learning with the intention of using that knowledge to transform ourselves into competent leaders—leaders with the ability to do the right thing for children by effecting real and lasting change.

Competence happens within four interdependent dimensions that must operate in tandem: technical competence, emotional competence, political competence, and developing competence in others.

Technical Competence

At its most basic level, technical competence is the knowledge and skills required to carry out a job or a task. In early childhood education, it is the ability to apply the principles, procedures, policies, and regulations of this industry in service to a larger vision of effecting positive change for children.

Technical competence requires mastery of the mechanics of your craft. Having a thorough understanding of the technical aspects of your work makes you an authority on the subject and lends you credibility in the eyes of others. It gives you the confidence you need to guide your colleagues and your organization, and it helps you avoid administrative pitfalls. Nobody wants to follow someone who doesn't know where he or she is going.

Leaders who have achieved technical competence are able to ask the right questions, such as the following: *What are the facts, figures, numbers, and data? Where is the supporting evidence? Where is the evidence that supports this as best practice? Has this practice been proven effective for the population we serve?* Technically competent leaders also support their actions and agendas through complementary competencies, including effective communication, consensus building, planning and organizing, and admitting and learning from mistakes.

However, technical competence alone can become a trap. Leaders can become preoccupied with following the rules. They then become restrained, unimaginative, and immobilized. In other words, they risk becoming what is known as a technocrat or, worse yet, a proceduralist. Transformational leaders who make lasting changes are individuals who are willing to break the rules and take risks when necessary. However, as I am quick to say to new and aspiring leaders, "You can't break the rules if you don't know them." Early childhood leaders need to understand and research the explicit and implicit rules of their discipline and their organization in order to decide which ones, once broken, might lead to a shift in thinking and in practice. In other words, once you learn the rules, you can figure out creative ways to break the rules in the areas that are most important to you and that could best lead to transformation. As Pablo Picasso stated, "Learn the rules like a pro, so you can break them like an artist."

There are many ways to develop technical competence, including on-the-job training, workshops and seminars, reading and studying, web-based research, and meetings and discussion groups on a specific topic. You can also develop a PPGP with a focus on specific technical competencies that you want to develop. Your PPGP should lay out how you will develop those competencies, along with a timeline for when you will complete each task. In order for leaders to realize their organizations' mission and goals, they must master the technical aspects of their work.

Emotional Competence

The second dimension of competence for a leader in early childhood education is emotional competence, also referred to as emotional intelligence or getting along with others. Emotional competence is the ability to understand your own feelings and emotions as well as those of the people around you in order to ensure the best outcome for each individual and for the organization as a whole.

In the book *Primal Leadership: Realizing the Power of Emotional Intelligence*, authors Daniel Goleman, Richard Boyatzis, and Annie McKee describe four components of emotional intelligence:

1. Self-Awareness (Emotional Self-Awareness): the ability to recognize and understand your moods, emotions, and drivers, as well as their effect on others
2. Self-Management (Self-Control): the ability to control or redirect disruptive impulses and moods—to suspend judgment, to think before acting
3. Social Awareness (Empathy): the ability to understand the emotional makeup of other people—to respond with skill to diverse groups of people according to their emotional makeup and their culture
4. Relationship Management (Inspiration): the ability to inspire and create a compelling vision of a shared mission—to make work exciting, to be proficient in managing relationships and building networks—an ability to find common ground and build support

Knowing yourself and knowing how to interact with others—often referred to as the soft skills—are two basic pillars and practices in the field of early childhood education. However, the hard truth about the soft skills is that they can make or break a leader's professional trajectory. Many individuals who are smart, sharp, and technically competent move willingly or are thrust from the classroom to the leadership table and fail miserably simply because they are lacking sufficient emotional intelligence. Because leaders set the emotional tone of their organizations, it is important that they develop emotional competence in order to minimize the conflicts, misunderstandings, stress, and fears that are counterproductive to their organizations' visions and missions.

If you have a high level of emotional intelligence, you are keenly aware of your emotional triggers as well as the triggers of the people around you, and you know how to engage with others in ways that draw them toward a common purpose—that of building a respectful and honest professional learning community. In this community, the components of emotional intelligence are acknowledged and referenced in professional conversations and reflections.

As powerful a competence as emotional intelligence can be, it is possible to take it to extremes. Leaders can become so engaged and self-absorbed in over-analyzing every human interaction that they reach a point of analysis paralysis, which results in organizational chaos.

To avoid this situation, leaders should engage in what I call "personal work" by placing focus on improving their own level of emotional intelligence. For example, to improve your self-awareness, make a list of what you perceive to be your strengths and weaknesses. Revisit your core values and be willing to hold yourself accountable to your track record. Be slow to speak and slow to anger. In terms of empathy, try to put yourself in someone else's place and listen and respond to the other person's feelings. And for social skills, work on your communication and conflict-resolution skills. Never hesitate to praise others for a job well done.

Political Competence

The third dimension of competence for an early childhood leader is political competence, or political savvy. Political competence is the ability to turn good ideas into action by leveraging the energy and support of others in order to accomplish your goals. According to Samuel B. Bacharach in his book *Get Them on Your Side*, "Political competence is the ability to understand what you can and cannot control, when to take action, anticipate who is going to resist your agenda, and determine whom you need on your side to push your agenda forward. Political competence is about knowing how to map the political terrain, get others on your side, and lead coalitions."

Your political competence is your ability to understand and influence the interrelatedness of trends and patterns at the local, national, and international levels that could have an impact on your organization's forward movement.

When I refer to politics in this field, I am not talking about classroom politics, center-based politics, or office politics. I'm talking about transformational leadership that happens on a local, national, and even international stage.

To have political competence, you must let go of the naive notion that politics is a dirty word or something evil to be avoided. To the contrary, politics is a significant part of the context in which we must conduct our leadership work, and it is an important realm to work in if we are to do the right thing and achieve the best results for children.

When you have political competence, you search out win-win situations by not making winning a zero-sum game. You are able to manage and sell your vision and ideas to those who are above, below, and around you in your organization. This is accomplished through offering a clear and compelling vision of the future, communicating effectively, building networks and coalitions, and engaging in personal conversations with others to hear their ideas and to gauge what they are thinking.

However, it's possible to be too political. Political savvy can easily become manipulative and self-serving, particularly when winning becomes the name of the game or comes at the cost of compromising your core values. Effective leaders are known by their brands—by what people think and say about them. Becoming overly political and indifferent to the needs and aspirations of others is what give politics a bad name.

When you have developed political competence, you have answered the following two questions to your satisfaction: *Why do you want to lead? What is the purpose of your leadership journey?* You have also mastered the arts of listening, reflecting on trends and patterns that could possibly impact your organization, and strategizing on how to build coalitions and networks to support your goal of doing the right thing for children.

Developing Competence in Others

The fourth dimension of competence for early childhood leaders is developing competency in others. Competent leaders seek to develop other competent leaders.

In their book *Multipliers: How the Best Leaders Make Everyone Smarter*, Liz Wiseman and Greg McKeown describe the five attributes of leaders who breed new, competent leaders:

1. They attract and optimize talent.
2. They require people's best work and best thinking.
3. They challenge people to stretch themselves.
4. They encourage rigorous debate.
5. They invest in other people's success.

The authors refer to this leadership style as "the multiplier effect." Leaders with the multiplier effect share and exploit the knowledge and brilliance that already exist within their organizations. A "multiplier" leader believes that people are smart in various ways, and that it is his or her job to find that potential and to maximize the smartness of those within the organization. Multiplier leaders work hard to develop and promote the knowledge, skills, and intelligence of others, thereby creating a community of competence that does more to further the interest of children than one individual could ever hope to do on his or her own.

By contrast, the authors describe another leadership style that they refer to as "the diminisher effect." Leaders who are diminishers deplete all of the knowledge and brilliance that exist within an organization and believe that all wisdom and knowledge comes from only them. Diminishers hold the view that people are born smart or dumb and that there is no value in attempting to mine for any innate intelligence.

Multipliers can sometimes slip into the role of diminisher because they have misread their organization's readiness for change. As a consequence, they are blinded by their own energy and enthusiasm, and they move forward before the team has rallied around their vision. The reluctance of their team members then inspires negative feelings in them about the people they are leading. Call on your emotional competence to help you navigate situations such as this one.

You can develop competency in others in a multitude of ways. Become a talent scout and search high and low, inside and outside your organization, for underdeveloped talent. Begin to ask yourself and those who work with you deep, provocative, open-ended questions that dig beneath the surface of appearances. Promote and encourage debate and creative tension in your organization. Stop trying to solve problems on your own—bring the discussion closer to the people who are affected by the issue, and let them have a go at it.

Whole Competency

These four core aspects of competence are achieved with practice over time. They are also interdependent. Embodying only three of the four aspects of competence will eventually undermine your leadership ability. If you are technically competent but don't take other people's feelings into account, you will lack a united team to push your agenda. By the same token, if you are emotionally competent but do not have the ability to execute your plans, you will be unable to gain the respect of those you are leading.

If you have emotional and technical competence but ignore political competence, you run the risk of being irrelevant, and leaders with greater political savvy may outmaneuver you. And if you refuse to develop competence in others in favor of doing everything yourself, you will burn out.

You may be smart and capable, but without all four aspects of competence in your leadership tool kit, you will not be able to effect transformational change as a leader in this field. Learn them diligently. Then, learn to apply them to your early education leadership agenda at the personal, organizational, and classroom levels.

Competence at the Personal Level

At the personal level, competence involves continual participation in the learning process and the active application of new knowledge in one's day-to-day life.

From a technical standpoint, a substantial amount of personal competence is devoted to mastering and practicing one's craft. There can be no resting on laurels here: a strong leader always knows that he or she does not know enough. Nor is knowing, in itself, enough. One must then take the knowledge and use it to experiment—to play around with it. Take the knowledge, adapt it and apply it for the current situation. In short, competence at this level comes from seeing your work as a practice, and then actually practicing it. You assume responsibility for gathering more knowledge of your craft, and then you use it to improve yourself. The more your technical competence improves, the more effective you become as an advocate for children.

The emotional aspect of competence at the personal level involves expanding and using your knowledge of others and your respect for them. You need to focus on your own receptivity in your interactions with people, regardless of age or background. If you're caring for a baby, what is your attitude toward that baby? When the baby starts to cry, do you shush it, or do you respect his or her inability to talk by asking, "What's wrong?" Emotional competence at this level revolves around a heightened personal awareness of the way you listen and respond to the individuals around you.

The competency of understanding politics at the personal level is connected to enacting the social-justice leadership quality. Helping children is not a disembodied ideal. It is a reality that stems from a personal desire to take an interest in the welfare of others—to act on it. Many early childhood leaders shy away from politics. "I hate the politics of it," you hear them say. But we have a personal responsibility to attend to politics, because it does impact us as individuals. We care on a personal level about equality and social justice, and we cannot talk about those things without considering the political factor. That is why it behooves us to take a personal interest in events taking place at the state and national level.

At the personal level, one enables competence in self and others by being an active participant in the community. This involves the promotion of good ideas through engagement—not just teaching but learning from what others have to say as well. Just as your peers benefit from your competence, your own competence as a leader has the opportunity to expand through this method of interaction and exposure.

You practice competence by progressing through stages of knowledge and then turning that knowledge into action. You start with basic knowledge, follow with procedural knowledge, and conclude with practiced knowledge. We can return to the example of being with a baby for a moment. Imagine walking into a house where the people caring for a baby were not aware that they should wash their hands before and after changing the baby's diaper. You start with basic knowledge and explain why that act of hygiene is important. Then you move on to procedural knowledge—the "how to." You share the knowledge of each step of changing the baby's diaper in a hygienic fashion. Finally, the knowledge becomes practice when it is put to use changing the diaper. Your personal competence on the technicalities of diapering enabled you to create competence in the baby's caretakers. That's how competence becomes a practice.

One risk of cultivating competence at the personal level is that of arrogance. Leaders sometimes become so competent that they believe there is nothing else for them to learn. As time goes on and your competence grows as a result of diligent practice, the ego can sometimes slip in and get a foothold. On the one hand, there is no shame in accepting acknowledgment for your achievements. On the other, we as leaders need to be wary of thinking that we are more competent than we actually are. Doing so may lead us to take on more than we can handle, which can in turn undermine our long-term goals. We must practice intellectual honesty, intellectual humility, and intellectual curiosity. There is always more to learn, and we should always be curious to find out what it is. When we continue to learn, we can continue to push ourselves to ever-higher levels of competency at the personal level.

Ultimately, competence at the personal level comes back around to perfecting your way of thinking, your way of seeing the world, your approaches to challenges, and your disposition with regard to setbacks. When you are operating at your best in these areas, you are prepared to take your skills to the next level.

Competence at the Organizational Level

Building strong competence at the organizational level is a requirement for any leader in the field of early childhood education. Organizational competence is one of the most powerful tools available to us when it comes to effecting positive change for children. It empowers us to bring the levers of power and influence into our control, which we can then use to bring transformational change to the lives of children and their families. Policy is formulated and carried out at the organizational level, and that makes this level of leadership the one with the highest potential to affect the greatest amount of change in the system. This is where decisions are made that impact the lives of everyone involved in the education system. The more competent a leader is at the organizational level, the more opportunity he or she has to create coherent and congruent policies that improve the lives of children.

From a technical standpoint, competence at this level requires us to fully understand every nook and cranny of how organizations work—both our own and those that affect us. A competent leader must know what needs to be done to keep his or her organization running smoothly, and he or she must take action accordingly.

In addition, a competent leader must employ a keen sense of analysis when it comes to understanding the workings of the systems in which he or she is operating. Ask yourself: *Which strategies are most effective? Which can be improved?* Where improvement is necessary, critical thinking must come into play. Technical competence at this level includes using your cultivated knowledge of people and processes to come up with lasting solutions to problems that will right the ship and keep things running smoothly within the organization.

From a socio-emotional perspective, a leader's organizational competence applies to facilitating relationships among one's staff. Tensions between coworkers are inevitable and can be damaging to the progress of a common goal. As leaders, it is our job to understand the varying perspectives and circumstances of those we work with and then to assist others in grasping those things as well. We have to be sensitive to the cultural aspects of diverse populations. That might involve taking the needs of second-language learners into account; it might mean paying careful attention to the needs of those with disabilities. We cultivate this sensitivity in others by practicing it ourselves and leading by example. By resolving sensitive conflicts and promoting cultural competency within our organizations, we facilitate strong bonds and relationships, creating a team that is united in its goal of furthering the interests of children.

The organizational level of competence is where we have the opportunity to wield the greatest amount of leverage from a political point of view. This is where the action happens: city council, state assembly, and national government. This is where we as leaders need to work on advocacy and engagement. Advocacy is asking, *What do you care about? How do you want to leave the world? What do you want to contribute, and how can you use political systems to help you make those contributions?* Engagement is asking, *How, when, and where can you engage yourself in political organizations to effect positive change for children? How will you push and pull the levers of power to further your leadership agenda?*

Politics have a direct impact on our educational institutions; after all, it is government agencies that establish many of the rules and regulations that early childhood programs have to abide by. And the consequences of those rules and regulations are passed down to the children in our care. Therefore, we as leaders have a serious responsibility to know which politicians and laws will harm or help our organizations and to be involved in supporting political initiatives and candidates who will help us further our goals for children.

Effective leaders need to stay ahead of the game on this. We need to read the future to some extent in order to manage our agendas. Just because the mayor in power now happens to be a champion for your early childhood program does not mean that you can relax on the political front. When the next election rolls around, the sands may shift, and you need to position yourself to ensure that you are not excluded from the notice of whoever the next round of leaders may be.

Of course, leaders at the organizational level have a responsibility to enable competence in others. This translates into promoting the active exchange of ideas among your team members. For leaders, this requires listening as well as teaching. Search for like-minded people and build a community of people who share your goals. Find opportunities to step outside your comfort zone. Attend teacher forums, directors associations, and professional conferences, such as the ones put on by NAEYC and their affiliates. Bring new people into the fold, and bring new ideas back to the fold as well. Keep in mind that as your staff members have the opportunity to learn from your knowledge and experience, you too have the opportunity to learn from theirs.

Another aspect of encouraging competence in one's organization is providing aspiring leaders with the opportunities to develop their skills. For instance, when my lab-school director was developing her leadership repertoire, I made a point of enrolling her in the conferences and seminars that I myself was planning to attend, such as a multiple-intelligences program for emerging leaders at Harvard. She has since passed on her knowledge gained at these conferences to several others in our lab school, making our entire team stronger.

By doing these things, you as a leader are not necessarily the well from which all competence is drawn. Rather, you are the spark that ignites the engine that drives the awareness that increasing competence is valued and revered throughout your organization.

Competence at the Classroom Level

At the classroom level, competence encompasses both creating a fair and comprehensive learning experience for children and inspiring this core value in children themselves.

First and foremost, competent teachers possess mastery of the teaching-learning process. I use the term *teaching-learning* because good teachers are constantly learning as much from their students as they are teaching them. There is an art and a science to teaching, and competence at the classroom level requires proficiency in both.

What is the art of teaching? Teaching as an art stems from practice, research, reflection, and action. Competent teachers do not leave questions unanswered.

They research solutions, and then they act on the solutions they unearth. Each child is unique, and each child is worthy of research and reflection. One size does not fit all. Competent teachers take this into account, and their style of teaching reflects it.

Socio-emotional competence is also critical at the classroom level. In order to help children achieve their full potential, teachers must be able to understand the diverse backgrounds and experiences that their students are coming to them with. Then, the teachers must take that understanding a step further and adjust their methods to accommodate those students' learning needs accordingly.

Political competence at the classroom level means connecting yourself to the larger systems that ultimately affect your work. If you want to change things, you have to get involved in the political system at some level. That may mean joining an existing teacher's organization or being a part of a teacher's interest forum. That may also mean creating some type of professional learning community with other like-minded individuals who want to do the right thing for children. Connect with other people who are concerned about the same issues. Then, don't just sit around and complain. Take the initiative to form a coalition or a collaborative that will take action for your cause. When you engage in acts of social activism on behalf of young children you are demonstrating and exercising political knowledge and skill at the classroom level.

Leaders who are not teaching in the classroom play a major role in promoting competence at the classroom level. They set the tone, expectations, culture, and attitudes that create a high-performing, highly effective teaching environment. The leader can make or break a teacher's willingness and ability to do the right thing for children by embracing new and engaging curriculum ideas and practices and by becoming a thoughtful, reflective, and effective early childhood practitioner. To make this happen, first and foremost the leader must lead by example in everything he or she says and does. The leader must keep the vision, values, and passion at the forefront of everything—the classroom cannot be the teacher's private domain and fiefdom without any interaction with the leader. Therefore, leaders must practice the art of management by spending an inordinate amount of time in and around the classroom in order to figure out which of a teacher's competencies require further development.

Finally, great leaders inspire and promote confidence among children and adults. Encourage, don't discourage. Find what's right instead of focusing on what's wrong. Return to your fundamental belief in human potential, and seek to maximize the potential in every person who comes into your circle of influence.

Cultivating Competence

Use the following questions as a starting point to begin—or continue—cultivating the core value of competence:

1. What effective leadership competencies do I already have?
2. What effective leadership competencies do I need to develop?
3. What am I doing to systematically develop leadership competencies in others?
4. What am I doing to ensure that my leadership walk matches my leadership talk?

Competence in Action

Ultimately, the full quality of competence is greater than the sum of its parts. Competence is the type of action that transcends particularities and simply makes a difference for the better. Figuratively speaking, when you can teach a group of children in the brush with no lesson plan and nothing more than ten sticks and five stones at your disposal, you have more than mastered this core value; you have made it a part of you. That is the way that it is meant to work. That is how you do the right thing for children.

Fun and Enjoyment

People rarely succeed unless
they have fun in what they are doing.

Dale Carnegie

A broken spirit cannot lift another broken spirit. In the early childhood field, we are really about much more than just education. We are about human development. Development springs from a willingness to learn. And nothing fuels a willingness to learn like the knowledge that you are going to have fun doing it.

Fun is important because it helps us to reduce stress and tension. Fun opens us up to different ways of thinking, stirs our creative juices, and stimulates our imaginations. When we are enjoying ourselves, our minds naturally open up to new possibilities and ideas. In the spirit of fun, we adopt a more positive attitude. We give ourselves permission to be more playful and to wonder about and explore things that we might have dismissed as silly or impossible otherwise. The power of discovery becomes limitless.

And that's only the beginning. Once our attitude has been recast in the light of enjoyment, the nature of the word *work* changes. Its demands become less daunting, and its rewards more bountiful. Those who enjoy their work rarely require outside motivation, because their motivation lies within them. They see their work as special and noble, and they walk with lightness in their steps and with purpose in their hearts.

From a leadership perspective, the core value of fun and enjoyment energizes people and inspires them to do the right thing for children. By indulging in it yourself, you become an inspiration to those around you. High energy translates into high motivation, which in turn leads to high innovation, and finally to high mobilization. I can't count the number of people who have attended my workshops or had a discussion with me in person, caught the fun and enjoyment bug, and called me a short time later to report—with amazement in their voices—that lately they'd been finding themselves on the phone well beyond work hours doing their part to improve early childhood education. I've reminded them to have fun and to bring humor into the work place. And now they're not just doing the work because they have to make a living, they're doing it because it's fun and enjoyable.

Interestingly enough, even the military with its tradition of spit and polish, efficiency, preciseness and discipline, also places a high premium on humor. According to the study "Humor and its Implications for Leadership Effectiveness," by Robert F. Priest and Jordan E. Swain published in *Humor: International Journal of Humor Research* in 2002, the United States Army leadership manual views having a good sense of humor as an important leadership trait. The study showed that there is a correlation between humor and leadership effectiveness.

I know this to be true: effective leaders create a space for fun in the workplace by modeling energy and enthusiasm for the work that they do. It is the leader's joyous enthusiasm that motivates others to always do their personal best. The leader's joyous energy is contagious and it sends a cue to others on how to act and how to have fun. The leader's nonverbal message when things get tough is "nothing saves you like a sense of humor." Humor can serve to diffuse tense situations in the workplace and rally individuals around their shared mission and vision. However, humor should always be used appropriately and never at the expense of any individual or group.

Effective leaders use humor to show the absurdity of many of our thoughts, words, and deeds. They establish a mind-set and a set of behaviors that permeates throughout their organization by exhibiting an upbeat approach to the multitude of challenges that arise. It is the leader's responsibility to create a work environment that is "playful" not "play-less"—an environment that motivates others to explore and release their creative energy, experiment with quirky ideas, and make mistakes while having fun.

Employing this core value as a leader also means appreciating and accepting people for who they are. Not everyone is going to think and work the way you do. Not everyone is going to approach their work with mirthful enthusiasm. There's no point in tearing your hair out trying to change that. You can't change it. What you can do is enjoy the spectrum of personalities and experiences that your colleagues bring to the table and learn to laugh at your own eccentricities in the way that you react to the situations you find yourself in. You can walk the light edge of finding the humor in things even when something is going wrong. You can step back and learn to see the fun and the enjoyment associated with the work. When you do, you promote learning—not only for yourself but also for those in your organization, adults and children alike.

Everyone comes with a natural personality. That personality probably isn't going to change very much. However, the core value of fun and enjoyment is something that can be cultivated in just about anyone. You can develop a positive disposition, and as a leader you can help others develop it too. We're here, so we might as well enjoy it. Let's do everything in our power to lift our own spirits and, in the process, lift the spirits of those around us as well.

Fun and Enjoyment at the Individual Level (Unearthing Your Inner Child)

People often say to me, "You are always upbeat." That isn't true. If it was, I'd be simpleminded. However, there is one conscious thing I do that invariably gives people this impression: I always approach my work life and my personal life with a sense of fun and enthusiasm.

Drawing the core value of fun and enjoyment out in the workplace begins with drawing it out of yourself. You have to create personal space that is fun and balanced. That doesn't necessarily mean that you're laughing every minute of every day. However, nothing saves you from exhaustion and defeat like a sense of humor. Finding humor in everyday situations and in the irony of things you say or do is a very effective way to increase your fun and enjoyment quotient. We each have the responsibility—and the joy—of unearthing what fun and enjoyment means to us as individuals.

At the individual level, enjoyment is the counterbalance to the misplaced negativity every one of us inevitably encounters in this field. You are going to have days when you cross paths with people who are not doing the right thing for children. When that happens, you have two choices. You can get angry about it and fuel the negativity further. Or you can act to the best of your ability within your circle of control by staying focused on your own positive contribution to your organization and to the field of early childhood education as a whole. Cultivating your own sense of fun and lightheartedness makes it easier to weather these storms when they come rolling in.

When you have a strong personal sense of fun and enjoyment, you can use this leadership quality as a tool for self-analysis and reflection. Specifically, you can use it to react to the things that happen around you in a way that promotes knowledge and growth. A leader who has a solid grasp of this leadership quality is able to look him or herself in the mirror when plans go amiss and say, "Wow, that was a real hoot. I was pushing something that did not need to be pushed. I was part of the reason that communication broke down and all along I thought that I was communicating superbly." When you can laugh at yourself and your reactions to other people, you become much better equipped to deal with daunting situations. Developing a sense of humor and lightheartedness in the workplace is a powerful tool for coping with stress, dealing with conflict, and managing deadlines and failures. You are not afraid to deconstruct your own failures and see where they went wrong. Instead, you are able look straight into the eye of failure and laugh, because you know that failure is a part of learning, growing, and succeeding.

Approaching yourself and your work with a light touch is contagious. Others can sense the positive energy you're exuding. They see you having fun, and they want to be part of that. As a leader, the fun and enjoyment you take in your work is the battery that powers your organization. I myself approach life this way, and the effects of it are visibly present every single day in my environment. People get a clear message from me, without my ever saying a word: "Things are going well. We can make this happen. We can do incredible things together."

And sure enough, we do.

Fun and Enjoyment at the Organizational Level

John Naisbitt notes in his book *Reinventing the Corporation*, "Many business people have mourned the death of the work ethic in America. But few of us have applauded the logic of the new value taking its place: 'Work should be fun.' That outrageous assertion is the value that fuels the most productive people and companies in this country."

Now and then, I am asked to share my experiences as a leader with large groups of people. Sometimes there are two thousand of them gathered in a huge auditorium. More often than not, they have certain expectations of what they are about to bear witness to. After all, they are serious administrators and serious teachers attending a serious gathering. They expect to hear a serious presentation about the serious challenges that we face in early childhood education spoken in a serious tone of voice by a serious man.

On such occasions, I take particular pleasure in stepping up to the microphone, opening my mouth, and singing, "Hello, hello, hello, and how are you?" to them. Needless to say, it doesn't take them long to figure out that they're not in for just another boring speech.

I do in my speeches what I do in my daily role as a leader, which is to say I take the tension out of the air and give the people I'm working with permission to smile. The core value of fun at the organizational level revolves around this concept. As leaders, we need to draw on our own sense of fun and enjoyment to create an environment where people can think outside the box and realize their visions for greatness.

Heaviness in the workplace is an enormous handicap to what we are trying to collectively achieve in early childhood education. We want our children to grow up curious, fearless, and eager to explore. Yet when we as adults work in an organization that is too straitlaced and stuck on rules, we ourselves cannot embody these values. We are reluctant to try new ideas for fear that we'll be punished. The result is a stagnant system in which nothing is ever challenged, and therefore nothing ever improves.

As leaders, we must strive to put wonderment and joy back into the workplace. It is time to dispel the myth that a serious, all-business approach is the only or even the best way to get things done. The reality is that this approach is neither of those things. It is more than simply possible to be driven toward a mission while still being lighthearted in your work—it is ideal. Whereas a person who works without joy has a finite amount of energy to put toward his or her goal, that person's joyful counterpart draws on a well of passion to continually fuel his or her activities. The result is that not only do things get done faster but also they get done better and with more innovation than is the case with the traditional model.

Creating a work environment that people want to come to every day is not as simple as throwing office parties on Friday afternoons. The idea is not to come up with ways for individuals to enjoy themselves by skirting around the work. The idea is to come up with ways to encourage people to have fun doing the work itself. When we create environments that are constantly on the lookout for new forms of fun, we promote new and creative ideas and new ways of doing things. We also create a setting that inspires those we lead to do their personal best every day, in every way. We as leaders then reap the reward not only of a stronger organization but also of watching those under our mentorship rise to their full potential as human beings.

Inspiring adults, as much as children, to succeed is a key part of this core value at the organizational level. As a leader, you cannot be an antagonist in the way you interact with people. If you're flexible and if you have a playful personality, you can use that to bring out the best in everyone around you. If you are constantly striving to find the fun, humor, and lightness in the challenges your organization is facing, then you will invite participation, and your team will solve problems more efficiently. By contrast, if you dwell on the negative, the odds are high that you're going to be dealing with those challenges on your own rather than with a team of smart and willing collaborators. Promoting fun and enjoyment in intra-organizational relationships has the power to transform a humdrum group of individuals into a positive, high-energy team united to accomplish a common goal. The stability that this kind of teamwork lends to an organization is everything we could ask for as leaders, and then some.

I once hosted a leadership workshop for one hundred principals. Most of them walked in the door with straight faces and not a laugh line in sight. No doubt they were expecting some well-structured bullet-pointed lists on ideal methods for executing strong leadership in an educational environment.

Instead, I sat them down and said, "I want each of you to come up with a headline you'd like to read about yourself in your local newspaper. You've got one minute. Go."

They glanced at me and then at each other in surprise for a moment. Then they started scribbling, and the true learning—not to mention the fun—began.

Fun and Enjoyment at the Classroom Level

Without question, the biggest obstacle to achieving fun and enjoyment at the classroom level is the notion that teachers must have absolute control over their students at all times. Think about this for a minute. *How many things in your life do you have absolute control over* anything *at all times*? If you're like most of us, the answer to that question is probably not too many. How absurd, then, is the very concept of trying to maintain that kind of control over twenty different four-year-old lives in a single room at the same time for six hours or longer every day? You'd have better luck hanging the moon!

To promote the core value of fun and enjoyment in the classroom without surrendering everything to chaos, we as educators need to exchange the idea of having control over students for the concept of developing relationships with them. When we do this, a whole new dynamic blossoms between teachers and the children in their care. Just like adults, children don't like being forced to do things. They want to participate in activities of their own free will. When you show an interest in them, they respond by showing an interest in you as well. The result of this bond is a level of cooperation that not only gets things done but allows for fun and enjoyment to flourish in the process.

A new lab-school teacher recently came to speak to me and the director for advice. "I don't know what I'm doing wrong," she confessed, exasperated. "The children just don't respect me. It isn't because I'm new either," she insisted. "John hasn't been here much longer than I have, but they love him. I don't get it. What's wrong with me?"

I looked her in the eye. "The reason John is doing better is because we've been coaching him on how to take things in stride," I said, as the director nodded in agreement. "When he first started, every time he opened his mouth it was to give an order. 'Hey Daren, don't do that. Why are you over there?' Every time I walked into his room, all I wanted to do was pick up a stick of Elmer's and glue his mouth shut." The new teacher cracked a little smile. "My point being," I went on, "you can't get on kids' cases for every little thing. Letting them explore is part of their natural growth process. Children are supposed to break rules. They're supposed to test the limits. If we crack down on them for every tiny detail, we limit their development."

"So you're saying I should . . . I should . . ." she started.

"I'm saying you should lighten up," I summarized simply. "Don't be so serious all the time. Keep yourself in the moment. Kids can sense when you're not really present mentally. You have to engage them and take part in what they're doing and saying. Be curious about them. Develop caring and light-hearted relationships with them. That's when they'll start to listen to you."

Like so many other new teachers, she learned firsthand that any time you have to tell children, "I am the teacher," you're in trouble. Because the truth is that you're not the teacher. They are their own teachers, and it is our job to provide them with the environment and the opportunities to learn. Teachers must learn to lighten up and to give children options. Instead of worrying about children who break the rules, we should worry about children who *don't* break them. Why aren't those children exploring and trying new things? Are we doing something that's making them afraid to come out of their shells? A teacher who embodies fun and enjoyment inspires those same things in his or her students as well. Where that core value goes, rule breaking is sure to follow. Learning, growth, recognition, and fulfillment are sure to follow too.

Cultivating Fun and Enjoyment

Proactively cultivate fun and enjoyment in yourself and others by taking the following questions into consideration:

1. Are you modeling a passion and enjoyment for the work that you do? If so, how? If not, what can you do to change your approach?
2. Have you created customs and rituals that symbolize your vision and mission and promote fun and group cohesiveness?
3. How are you creating and maintaining fun and enjoyment activities for you and the staff?
4. What is the measurement of the fun and enjoyment index of the staff? What can you do to raise that measurement?
5. Are you spotlighting and rewarding excellence?

Catching Flies

"You catch more flies with honey than you do with vinegar" is one saying that absolutely applies to any leader who wants to do the right thing for children.

The best leaders are the ones who have fun doing what they do. Likewise, the best organizations are the ones whose participants have a shared notion of enjoyment and mirth. And anyone who has ever heard a child squealing with uncontainable laughter has proof enough that this core value lies at the heart of leading a rich and fulfilling life.

When we bring the energy and enthusiasm that fun generates into the work-place, we promote more than just learning and growth. We promote happiness. There is nothing we can give to ourselves, to our coworkers, or to our children that holds higher value than that.

Personal Renewal

As human beings, our greatness lies not so much in being able to remake the world . . . as in being able to remake ourselves.

Mahatma Gandhi

It had been a long week. An important contract we needed to support our organization's professional-development work had been delayed due to some bureaucratic snafu. We were one teacher short at the lab school, which meant that we were out of compliance with the licensing requirements. On top of that, a report that was commissioned by a local early childhood advocacy group that I was a member of had just been released and stated that the infant-toddler care in the District of Columbia was at a low level of quality.

I was at the office trying to come up with new curriculum ideas for the lab school that linked with the district's newly revised early learning standards, but it was no use. My brain felt as though it had turned to brick in my skull. I was stuck and going nowhere fast. Emotional frustration and intellectual fatigue were getting the better of me. So I pushed curriculum brainstorming out of my mind.

It was time to do something else.

An idea rose to the surface of my thoughts. Several days ago, a friend had mentioned an article in the paper about the Textile Museum. The museum had a new exhibit on Southeast Asian textiles that explored how geographically close communities distinguished their ethnic identity through the use of patterns, colors, and techniques. It sounded very appealing. True, it had nothing to do with curriculum standards for three- and four-year-olds—but on a purely personal level, my interest was piqued.

I grabbed my jacket and headed for the door.

A short time later, I was treading through halls filled with ancient and contemporary silk brocades and cotton batiks. Warm light cast itself over featured pieces: tapestries, hip wraps, scarves, ikats, and wall hangings. The ambiance alone was enough to revive the sluggish synapses in my head. I found myself reflecting on the incredible fact that all of this elaborate creativity had its root in simple, natural fibers. The fact that these fibers could generate such rich beauty was inspiring to me.

Before long, my thoughts took on a life of their own, leading me down the paths of my previously acquired knowledge: the terrible history of the Silk Road and the complex cultures of Southeast Asia, where the pieces I was viewing were inspired by or hailed directly from. Finally, a thought wandered in that should perhaps have been obvious to begin with.

Why not conduct a project at the lab school with a focus on clothing and textiles? Just like that, I had solved my curriculum problem from earlier in the afternoon. I walked out of the Textile Museum two hours later with an elevated spirit, already contemplating which parts of the history, process, and cultural roots of natural fibers, such as silk, cotton, and wool, we could explore with the children at the lab school.

The Significance of Personal Renewal

People expect great things from leaders. But we are all human. The physical, emotional, and intellectual acts of leadership can be quite demanding and draining. That is why the core value of personal renewal is so critical to leadership success.

Hopefully, we as leaders in early education love our work (if you do not, please read chapter 6 again). We love playing our part in doing the right thing for children. Being agents of change who make the educational experience better for young children and their families is incredibly rewarding for us. But we need to acknowledge that it takes a lot of energy—physical and mental—to do it well. Leveling the playing field for children from underresourced communities is hard work, and as such it requires quite a bit of intellectual and emotional capital on our part. This can be exhilarating when you achieve or are near achieving your goals and desired results. It can also be draining when your technical, emotional, and political competencies do not appear to produce your desired results. The leadership quality we use to cope with both the highs and the lows is personal renewal.

Personal renewal is the act of revitalizing yourself so that you are able to give your best to others consistently on an ongoing basis. Just as others are deserving of your aid and attention, you yourself are deserving of it too. Leaders should adhere to the advice that mental-health professionals often give to individuals who assume the role of primary caretaker for family members: first take care of yourself. Even the airline safety message goes, "If you have a small child traveling with you, secure your mask first before securing the child's." In each instance the admonition is that the best way of taking care of others is to take care of yourself.

In a way, leaders are caretakers. We are caretakers of vision. We are caretakers of strategy and the implementation of strategy. And, in early childhood we have the extra responsibility of being caretakers of the human spirit. The responsibility that comes with these goals and ideals is enormous, and it is impossible to bear the weight of it on our shoulders for long without seeing to the strength of the shoulders themselves in the first place.

Most people do not understand how to get out from under the weight of their work. They are so engrained in the process of producing results, meeting deadlines, and helping others fix their lives that they can sometimes forget that they have lives of their own to tend to. What they fail to understand is that this is a self-destructive pattern of behavior. If it goes on long enough, these individuals burn themselves out—at which point no results are produced, no deadlines are met, and no people are helped until personal recovery has taken place.

Personal renewal is about balance. It is about refilling your physical, emotional, spiritual, and intellectual buckets, all of which can become drained through ongoing acts of leadership. It is about finding the things in life that give you energy and then pushing that energy forward to improve the lives of others. According to Carisa Bianchi in *Unwritten Rules: What Women Need to Know About Leading in Today's Organizations* by Lynn Harris, "When people don't take time out, they stop being productive. They stop being happy, and that affects the morale of everyone around them." There is nothing wrong with being driven by your work. In fact, work needs to be an integral part of your life if you intend to be an exemplary leader in this field. Nevertheless, you also need to have things that are completely yours to offset it—meditation, exercise, artistic endeavors, social events—or you will lose your sense of identity, and your efficacy as a leader will suffer.

The wonderful thing about personal renewal is that it encourages creativity and passion. Taking the time to engage in activities that make you feel good physically, emotionally, spiritually, and intellectually helps you feel refreshed and reenergized, and when that happens you are at your personal best. When you are committed to your work, the creativity and passion you have outside your work ends up naturally spilling over into your work arena. In this way, by indulging in the things that bring you personal joy, you are ultimately improving the lives of others along with your own.

I often say that steel is the hardest of metals, yet even that crumples under certain destructive conditions. We as individuals face those destructive conditions in the form of stress every day. Personal renewal begins with the acknowledgment that you are human and that there are forces in the world that are greater than you. Draw upon them to reenergize yourself. Taking the time to do this may appear selfish on the surface, but the truth is that it enables you to be of maximum service to yourself and to others. This connects to what I call the head, hands, and heart of leadership.

The head of leadership is what we know about doing the right thing for children. It is what a leader does to increase his or her knowledge and skills about managing change creatively.

The hands of leadership are what we actively do to ensure that we are doing the right thing for children. They are the acts of leading by example that inspire others to do their personal best and to recommit to the organization's mission and vision.

The heart of leadership is what we do to improve upon what we are doing for children. It is what a leader does to increase his or her interpersonal effectiveness, creativity, and systems alignment in order to expand trust and synergy among the team as a whole. Viewed in that light, personal renewal and continual improvement are actually the ability to manage the head, hands, and heart of leadership with energy and aplomb.

Personal Renewal at the Individual Level

To draw people to you as a leader, you need to be able to effectively manage your physical, mental, and spiritual energy levels. This process begins with the acknowledgment that personal renewal and continual improvement are necessary in the first place. As simple as that may sound, we in the United States tend to have difficulty digesting this concept. The amount of unused vacation time that people in this country have is staggering. Some individuals actually calculate their retirement based on how much vacation time they have accumulated over the years. In my opinion, they are missing the point.

The reason we have paid vacation is to provide us with the opportunity for personal renewal. Other nations seem to have a clearer grasp of this idea. Europe all but shuts down for the entire month of August. Yet in the United States, we have taken our work ethic to such an extreme that it is throwing us out of balance and, ironically, diminishing our ability to reach our full potential.

Those who know me often comment that I work hard. I tell them that that's true—but I also play just as hard as I work. When I left the public schools after twenty-five years of service, the administration didn't owe me a single day of paid vacation. I pour my whole heart into my work during the school year, and I love to do that. But I always take the time to step away from my schedule throughout the year, and during the summer months I am physically gone—out of office and out of the city.

One place I like to go is a pristine island retreat south of Cape Cod in Massachusetts. My staff knows this. Whenever I get cranky or frustrated, they start mumbling that it's time for me to take a trip to my island. There, I am able to reclaim my inner spirit and become relaxed while getting reconnected with my true self and my core values. I appreciate the experience of communing with nature while sitting outside, rebooting my intellectual curiosity by reading good books, and enjoying the awe and wonderment of exploring the simple, natural beauty of my surroundings. Then when I return to work, I tend to drive my staff crazy with delight as I energetically off-load the scores of fantastic ideas that happened to come to me during my sojourn of personal renewal.

At the individual level, personal renewal is the search for inspiration and revitalization; personal renewal is the focused energy we use to inspire ourselves and others. From an external standpoint, we need to understand and accept the fact that it is okay to draw energy from others as well as give it to them.

On an internal level, we must learn to create time and space for ourselves that can be used for self-reflection and contemplation. The possibilities for how you use that time and space are bottomless and unique to you. Maybe it revitalizes you to explore new exhibits at museums, attend a lecture, take a random walk through your neighborhood, or take a planned walk through a park. Maybe venturing out into nature on a jog or on a bicycle puts you back in touch with yourself. Maybe you like to write, paint, meditate, or read a book of no redeeming social value. Maybe once in a while the only thing you really want to do is sleep in. A number of my good friends keep journals, which they say gives them the perspective they need to reflect on what they've done to make today successful so that they can do it again tomorrow.

Whatever the case, by engaging in activities that absorb us and bring us joy and pleasure on a fundamental level, we are really engaging ourselves in personal renewal. The end result of taking time to regenerate ourselves enables us to expand our own horizons, and the energy we draw from such experiences makes us stronger as individuals and as leaders.

Personal Renewal at the Organizational Level

At the organizational level, leaders promote personal renewal by engaging their staff in activities that inspire team members to delve into this leadership quality at their own individual level. As the saying goes, "A chain is only as strong as its weakest link," and it is the responsibility of a good leader to ensure that the chain is as strong as possible. For us that means that an organization can only be strong and high performing when all of its members feel a sense of renewal, rejuvenation, and recommitment to a set of common goals.

Leaders can sometimes be very egocentric. Many fall prey to the illusion that their organizations are all about them, when in fact nothing could be further from the truth. The success of our organizations is contingent upon our ability as leaders to form meaningful and enduring relationships with others. From that solid foundation, we must then do everything in our power to influence a positive way of thinking in our colleagues, as that will in turn influence the quality of the results that our organization as a whole is able to produce.

I would not consider it an exaggeration to say that personal renewal lies at the heart of positive thinking. It brings out the best in people, who are then able to contribute to the goals of the team at their highest level of potential. When we plant the seed of happiness, it can only follow that good things will grow from it.

When I was the director of early childhood programs for the DC school system, the other people in management and I organized a personal renewal retreat for thirty teachers and staff. We held it at the Airlie Center—a beautiful event center on 1,200 acres in Northern Virginia. In general, teachers don't always get to engage in a lot of grown-up behavior in the day-to-day activities of their jobs, and we wanted to give them the opportunity to explore their creativity in an adult context. We started with activities the children themselves participated in—such as building with blocks, playing with sand and water, and dancing, singing, and painting—for the sheer pleasure of enjoying the awe and wonderment of those childhood activities. Into each of these activities we incorporated a reflective activity where the teachers focused on how these experiences renewed them physically, emotionally, intellectually, and spiritually. And we asked them to consider the implications of their reflections: what would this experience mean for the way they approached their teaching?

The challenges we face in early education reform cannot be tackled by a lone individual. They cannot even be solved by a team with only average competence and passion. Orchestrating personal renewal within your organization is more than just a kind gesture—it is a strategy for moving our work forward in a way that benefits children, families, and the early childhood field at large.

Personal Renewal at the Classroom Level

Just like leaders and administrators, educators can also encounter burnout when they are not given time away from their work. Personal renewal at the classroom level aims to ensure that leaders promote reflection and rejuvenation among teachers and to encourage those teachers to pass on their healthy practices to the children in their care.

Personal renewal is very important at the classroom level, because our teachers are the individuals who directly connect with children on a day-to-day basis. Those children come to them from a variety of backgrounds and experiences, and they constantly present the teachers with new challenges. Keeping up with so many individual children all day requires an immense amount of energy in itself, and the demands on teachers don't stop there. There are times when the bleak circumstances of certain children's personal situations and the overall inertia of the education system can be frustrating, and progress toward change feels daunting and extremely slow.

Teachers must engage in personal renewal to stay hopeful and strong in the face of such challenges. Unshakable belief in themselves translates into unshakable belief in children, regardless of what zip code or income bracket the latter come from. Teachers who work hard at their craft are still bombarded with increased demands to implement what they deem developmentally inappropriate curriculum from administrators, families, and the public. Many teachers who participated in "the reading wars" of the 20th century now find themselves engaged in "the play wars" of the 21st century where the legitimacy of play in the early childhood classroom is being called into question.

All the noise in the teaching and learning environment can be demoralizing, and teachers can easily lose sight of their original calling to become a teacher of young children. When this happens, they may fall into a cycle of despair and begin to view the children and the children's families as the source of their discontentment. In some cases, this causes them to retire while they are still in the classroom. They have lost their passion to do the right thing for children.

By contrast, teachers who participate in personal renewal are never going to give up on children, because by staying in touch with their personal interests and passions, these teachers are able to keep their energy and focus at work on what they are trying to achieve—doing the right thing for children.

A good first step toward personal renewal for teachers is for them to get in touch with their inner child by thinking about and reflecting upon the sights, sounds, and pleasures of childhood. As a follow-up to the teacher retreat described earlier, the teachers who attended engaged in a book forum after they read two books: *Children's Letters to God* compiled by Stuart Hample and Eric Marshall and *Lessons from the Sandbox: Using the 13 Gifts of Childhood to Rediscover the Keys to Business Success* by Alan Gregerman. Additionally, the teachers took part in monthly professional development sessions, where they worked in small groups to analyze the thinking and motivation of children who asked such questions as, Does the man in the moon have a wife? Who makes the rain? Where does the snow go when it melts? Teachers maintained journals in which they wrote reflections. They also wrote about related experiences from their lives, such as a personal nature walk, a visit to the zoo or a children's playground, or a photo of something that created awe and wonderment for them, such as a sunrise, a waterfall, a rainbow, or newly fallen snow.

Inspiring personal renewal at the classroom level can be something as simple as using the afternoon nap period as a time to emotionally decompress by playing soothing music and relaxing your mind and spirit. Or, it could be taking a professional excursion to a new location, thereby encouraging participants of all ages to think outside the box and explore their creativity on new levels. In every case, it can only push us one step closer to achieving positive results for children.

Cultivating Personal Renewal

To proactively cultivate personal renewal in yourself and to encourage others to do so as well, consider the following questions:

1. Are you walking, talking, living, and breathing the mission and vision of your organization?
2. Are you pursuing an appropriate work-life balance by taking time to rejuvenate?
3. Have you taken time to reassess and recommit to your core beliefs and engage in honest self-reflection?
4. How do you focus your energy on strategies that align your organizational systems and empower staff to improve?

The Ladle and the Fountain

Leaders are the source of energy that others draw from in their search for inspiration. Without personal renewal, that energy is limited—like water in a bucket. With personal renewal, the bucket becomes a fountain, replenished from a bottomless source. Others come to us for ideas, for advice, and for help in fixing problems. Every time they do, a ladle of energy is taken from that source. It is therefore our responsibility to keep the source replenished. The true value of personal renewal is that it gives us a bottomless source to work from.

Is your source a bucket, or is it a fountain? When the answer is the latter, you have embodied this leadership quality, and you have the power you need to inspire others for years to come.

Perseverance

Patience and perseverance have a magical effect
before which difficulties disappear and obstacles vanish.

John Quincy Adams

When most people think of perseverance, they think of sayings like, "If at first you don't succeed, try, try again," or "When things get tough, the tough get going." Their parents and coaches used phrases like these to spur them on to success in school or to victory in a competitive sport. As with other clichés from a bygone era, most people don't give sayings like these much thought.

However, there is a growing body of research that views the noncognitive factors of grit, tenacity, and perseverance as critical factors for success in school and in life. If you want to read in-depth on this, check out *How Children Succeed: Grit, Curiosity, and the Hidden Power of Character* by Paul Tough or *Giving Kids a Fair Chance* by James J. Heckman. Simply stated, perseverance is the ability to accomplish long-term goals or visionary ideas amid challenges and setbacks. Viewed in that light, it seems our parents and coaches were on to something.

I often begin my speeches by quoting the two stanzas that follow from the poem "Don't Quit" by Edgar A. Guest. I think that just about everyone, at some point in their careers, has toyed with idea of giving up. It may have been the result of yet another bad interaction with a supervisor, colleague, or child who has plucked your last nerve or perhaps you just feel stuck in a rut. I find this poem to be inspirational and uplifting—it provides direction for those who are at a loss.

When things go wrong, as they sometimes will,
And the road you're trudging seems all up hill,
When the funds are low but the debts are high,
And you want to smile, but you have to sigh,
When care is pressing you down a bit,
Rest if you must—but don't you quit.

Success is failure turned inside out—
The silver tint of the clouds of doubt.
And you never can tell how close you are,
It may be near when it seems afar;
So stick to the fight when you're hardest hit—
It's when things seem worst that you mustn't quit.

The reason this poem has such resonance and provides comfort for me is because it speaks to a natural human tendency to give up when things get tough. I often say to my leadership students that leadership is hard and demanding. I tell them to expect some professional turbulence where there appears to be no calm air in sight. These challenges can push leaders to the brink of the valley of despair and cause them to question their effectiveness as leaders and the motives of those around them. However, the poem suggests that it is at this very juncture in the leadership journey that success may be within reach, and therefore we must hold fast to our hopes, dreams, and aspirations in order to overcome the desire to quit.

Defining Perseverance

Generally, people tend to hold a somewhat narrow view of what the term *perseverance* means. Ask anyone walking down the street to give you a definition, and you're liable to hear something along the lines of, "It's stick-to-itiveness," or "It means never giving up." Never giving up is indeed a key element of perseverance, however, it would be more appropriate to describe it as a strong will and desire to succeed and to not let setbacks keep you from attaining your goal. The other components of perseverance are grit—persisting in pursuit of your goal, mental toughness—an unshakable personal belief in your ability to accomplish your goal, and resilience—the ability to quickly bounce back from a setback.

Successful leaders must use perseverance intelligently. As useful as it may be, stick-to-itiveness can sometimes do more harm than good when we take it up blindly. Petitioning an uncooperative elected official day and night to pass legislation when that official is due to be replaced in a month with a new incumbent who already supports your cause, for instance, is one way that persistence might work against you. An effective leader understands that resources are always limited and finds smart ways to persevere in his or her goals. Why waste time and money petitioning an uncooperative official when you could put that same energy toward something that will yield results? Leaders need to make smart choices about when to persevere.

Another lens through which to look at perseverance as a leadership quality is how to turn failure into success. In this, we are again adding an element of strategy to the bare-bones concept of brute force. Not every plan we undertake is going to take us straight from point A to point B. Rather than persisting with a bad method when we have seen that it is not effective, it serves us better as leaders to find a creative way to turn the delay into a positive step forward.

I once had a wonderful idea to have our lab school host a national meeting of top experts in the field of early education. I envisioned that it would feature several well-known leaders in our field and that it would cover cutting-edge information on a slew of critical topics, including multiple intelligences, classroom design, materials, and curriculum. Everything was set to go: the public relations, the logistics, the speakers—many of whom had agreed to fly in from far-flung corners of the country to attend. Then I discovered, much to my dismay, that our registration was not going to support the cost of the project. I did everything I could within the bounds of reason to salvage it. When it became clear that my persistence was going to do more harm than good, however, I made the decision to call off the event.

But despite appearances, the day was not all lost. In the process of arranging it, I had formed new partnerships with many of these high-profile leaders who had agreed to speak. As I went through the process of refunding the cost of their travel expenses and providing them with the honoraria that had been promised, they told me, "This was such a wonderful idea. No one has ever done anything like it before. If you need me to help you out with it in the future, please let me know."

I thanked those big-name speakers and put their names on a list. When the circumstances change and the time is right to push this goal back to the forefront, I know that I have an all-star team waiting in the wings to make it happen. That is how a leader turns defeat into victory, and that is how to make perseverance work in your favor strategically in the long run.

Another aspect of perseverance that many people fail to recognize is the importance of focusing on the future as well as the present. It is always critical to set goals to give direction to your actions. However, it is equally important to be well apprised of the ground you are standing on. You as a leader need to be aware of situations when lofty goals and ideals are so far removed from the current reality that persistence alone is not going to be sufficient to bridge the gap.

That's not to say that lofty goals can never be achieved; only that there needs to be a more practical plan in place for achieving them. This goes back to intelligent perseverance. As leaders we must always engage in constant reflection on the cycle of setting a goal, planning its implementation, and executing that plan—then reassessing, replanning, rethinking, and re-executing it all over again as necessity requires. That is true perseverance in leadership.

Achieving your goals in the field of early childhood education will not happen overnight. Oftentimes the path is anything but linear and sequential. That is where we rely on perseverance to see us through. It is essential to think strategically. It is essential to celebrate small victories. And of course, it is essential to never give up.

Perseverance at the Personal Level

To persevere at the personal level is to engage in continual self-work, even when that work is hard to do. Nobody is perfect, and nobody ever will be. Nevertheless, it is the thirst for continual self-improvement that separates the average individual from the exceptional one.

Self-improvement can often be a monumental task. It is sometimes difficult even to acknowledge that we need improving let alone to take the initiative to make the necessary corrections. On an internal level, it may require examining our most fundamental beliefs with fresh eyes. On an external one, it may be defined as working toward professional excellence.

Oftentimes it happens that the internal and external levels of personal perseverance are connected. A fresh graduate may need to wade through any number of unpleasant jobs, narrow-minded bosses, and nonideal situations on his or her way up the professional ladder. Yet all the while, that new graduate is presented with the opportunity to learn from those adversities. Any experience, good or bad, should always provoke the question, "There is something for me to learn about myself here—what is it?"

The pursuit of mastery of one's craft is a key element of perseverance at the personal level. Achieving excellence is a great part of what enables us to guide others to excellence as well. More than that, however, continually engaging in this learning process inspires us to think outside the box. It pushes us to do things better, smarter, and faster than we did them before.

The key to perseverance at the personal level is having a vision and set of beliefs that inform your goals and focus your sights on your ideals. Perseverance is the ability to keep a larger vision in mind as you toil away at your craft. It is having a passion for action and a commitment to doing the right thing for children. It is accepting that life is not intended to be easy and that there will be bumps in the road along the way. Also, it is the realization that personal struggles and defeats create opportunities for growth and new learning. Finally, it is the ability to receive constructive feedback, to take time for self-reflection and self-renewal.

Ultimately, perseverance at the personal level builds tremendous strength of character. Those who are unwilling to give up on themselves are also those who are unwilling to give up on others, and that is one of the hallmarks of excellent leadership in early childhood education.

Perseverance at the Organizational Level

At the organizational level, perseverance is doing whatever is necessary to retool the early education system so that it is conducive to achieving the best outcomes for children. It is about keeping the focus on doing the right thing for children and not being deterred from your mission when you hit a rough patch. It is about knowing how and when to make a detour in order to get to your destination.

When I was the director of early childhood programs for the DC public-school system, I led a reform effort based on the conceptual framework of developmentally appropriate practices. In addition to more engaging and robust curriculum activities, the initiative promoted the idea of hands-on teaching across all the domains of learning. There were ample workshops and other training opportunities to ensure that these new ideas took root in the teachers' classrooms. Initially, there was some hesitancy toward the reform among the teachers and administrators. However, through carefully planned and frequent training and professional development, the teachers and administrators slowly but surely began to embrace this new way of organizing classrooms. Once things started moving in a positive direction, and once people began to understand that children do not all develop in a lockstep fashion and that there are myriad ways to help each child reach his or her full potential, I decided that it was time to introduce the concept of the multiage classroom.

The idea was that the age structure of schools—in which all three-year-olds were grouped together, four-year-olds were grouped together, and so on—was actually highly unnatural. You would never see a mother saying to her children, "I want my three-year-old over here." Moreover, all three-year-olds are not the same, nor are all seven-year-olds. It didn't make sense to expect them all to learn on the same schedule. By proposing the multiage initiative for the DC schools, our early childhood leadership team wanted to give children the gift of time. We wanted them to develop at their own pace and to be challenged according to their developmental level. We wanted the children to have continuity by having the same teacher over an extended period of time, and we wanted them to benefit from the richness of thoughts, ideas, and interactions that can happen when you mix ages, skills, talents, and dispositions.

However, transforming the multiage concept from a good idea into a reality took more than a handshake to achieve. The first line of rejection came from parents who were concerned that their children would lose out academically if they were put in a classroom where others were not as "gifted" as them. Then the teachers began to whine and complain about how it was already difficult to teach children of the same age with their varying degrees of ability—how in the heck could they take on the challenge of a multiage classroom? The next group to weigh in on the topic was the education subcommittee of the board of education. The committee members had serious reservations about the efficacy of this initiative. I was at my wit's end. The initiative was dead on arrival. It was time to regroup, rethink, and re-strategize.

In the months that followed, our early childhood leadership team engaged in extensive research, planning, and strategic thinking. We revisited our vision and our mission. We tested our assumptions as they related to our mission and vision, and we debated all of the pros and cons that came along with multiage classrooms. We conducted focus groups with teachers, and I personally went to the prospective pilot schools and held information sessions with parents.

Following that, we developed a revised proposal that included milestones and benchmarks we would encounter on the way to our goal. We presented the information to the superintendent for approval and then to the board of education. After all of that, we were granted permission to do a pilot test run of ten schools. Then came the phases of training the teachers, interacting with the parents, and instructing principals on how to manage the new structure. When the pilot schools saw success, the whole process began again as more and more schools began to switch over to the new methods.

By the time I was promoted from that position to deputy superintendent of the DC public schools, seventy-six out of 110 schools in the DC system had converted to the new multiage structure, and the rest were in the pipeline to make the transformation. Systemic change based on solid theory, research, and practice had been achieved. My core value of perseverance had transformed knowledge into a concrete result that was making a difference in the lives of hundreds of children.

Strategy has a powerful role to play in perseverance at the organizational level. Whenever possible, start with the end goal in mind and then work backward, analyzing the different ways that you can use available systems to achieve your aim. This allows you to build a plan that has a higher chance of success than if you had simply charged in blindly, which gives direction to perseverance and ultimately makes it that much easier for you to follow through with your goals.

Perseverance at the Classroom Level

Perseverance at the classroom level is simple: it means that you *never* give up on a child.

Leaders and teachers in the field of early education relentlessly pursue the common goal of competence of children. This begins with deconstructing our own preconceived notions and stereotypes about children themselves: what they can or cannot do and what they can or cannot learn. Every child learns in his or her own way, and as such the key to unlocking potential is different for each child. Taking down our mental barriers and discarding the old ideas that one size fits all when it comes to teaching is the first part of achieving the competence of every child in our care, regardless of background.

The second part is building on the things that a child is doing right rather than focusing on his or her difficulties. It falls to teachers to use the strengths of children to help them overcome their individual weaknesses.

When the classroom feels chaotic, many educators forget the importance of thinking about a child's behavior rather than reacting to it in the moment. Oftentimes a teacher will come to me complaining about the difficulties he or she is having with a student: he just can't learn his alphabet or she just won't pay attention in class. The first thing I always say to the teacher is, "I understand. Now, tell me one positive thing that this child is able to do from an academic or social-emotional standpoint."

Not infrequently, the teacher looks at me and says, "I can't think of anything."

To which I respond, "So is he disruptive all day long? When he comes in and says, 'Ms. Brown, I'm here,' is he hurling a block across the room, hitting Susie in the head? Tell me step-by-step what he does well."

Inevitably, there is always something good to be found. We pinpoint it, and we go from there.

In addition to the persistence that we as educators must demonstrate in pursuing the competence of our students, another aspect of perseverance at the classroom level is teaching this core value to the children themselves.

You may not think of a four-year-old as having perseverance. However, signs of it do begin to show themselves early in life. At the lab school, the gauge we use to measure a child's perseverance is referred to as task persistence. Does the child initiate tasks? Does he or she stay focused after the task has started? As simple as these questions may sound, they get at the heart of a much larger domain: self-regulation and executive functioning, both of which have their roots in the value of perseverance.

However, children need to have something to persevere for or toward—something that is worthy of their time, attention, and effort. They need a wide range of robust, engaging activities that honor their individual uniqueness and are intellectually challenging. They need to be given roots, wings, and the gift of time to pursue their interests and they need to know that they are valued and respected. They should be provided with everyday experiences that help them to understand that through struggle and effort they can achieve great things in school and in life.

Cultivating Perseverance

Begin—or continue—cultivating perseverance in yourself and others by considering the following questions:

1. Do you undertake change initiatives that are vision and mission driven?
2. Do you conduct research and consult with other leaders regarding the pros and cons of the change effort you plan to initiate?
3. How do you communicate to your staff and children that risk taking is encouraged and that they can learn from their failures?
4. In what ways do you foster an environment that encourages critical analysis and reflection on successes and failures, sprinkled with a little bit of humor?

The Power of Persistence

Perseverance as a leadership quality unfolds in multiple layers, and it applies to every level of leadership in early education. It is the determination that encourages us to overcome obstacles, yet its influence extends far beyond the boundaries of that basic definition as well. Perseverance at its best is intelligent and strategic. It helps us turn setbacks into advantages. Little by little, it allows us to change the inner workings of outdated systems for the better, helping us do the right thing for children.

But most of all, it pushes us to believe in children—no matter what.

Courage

Courage is what it takes to stand up and speak.
Courage is also what it takes to sit down and listen.

Winston Churchill

"Mr. Sykes, what happened to your foot?"

Twenty pairs of young eyes honed in on me, each of them silently echoing the same question. It was a Monday morning in the all-boys, ungraded primary classroom in Washington DC a few months into my first year as a teacher. Over the weekend, I had attended an after-hours party that became a tad raucous and had attracted the attention of the DC metropolitan police. Being a new teacher, all I could think of was the professional embarrassment and possible loss of my job as a result of being in a place where the police had been summoned. So in my panic, I made the mistake of jumping from a first-floor window and cutting my right foot—badly enough that I'd had to visit the hospital for stitches. I was in some pain and was walking with a severe limp.

This fact had not escaped my boys' notice.

Almost since I'd hobbled in the door, they had been asking me about my foot. At first I tried to put them off. I might be new, but I knew the rules: the children were not supposed to be exposed to anything even vaguely related to violence. It was the late sixties, and there were still very conservative, traditional ideas in place about how school teachers should conduct themselves in and out of school and what was appropriate information to share with children.

But my students' curiosity was stronger than all of my attempts to deflect their questions. Now here we were, sitting together on the floor for circle time—an event that called for sharing. And they were asking again.

This time, I paused and thought about the situation. After all, I reflected, these kids came from communities where shootings were practically a commonplace occurrence. Was a wound like mine really going to traumatize them? More than that, dodging their inquiry felt wrong to me.

I hesitated another moment, weighing my desire to be honest against the fact that I knew I could be risking my first real teaching job for this. Then I said, "Mr. Sykes was somewhere he should not have been, and I had to get out of there in a hurry. So I jumped out of a window and cut my foot pretty badly. They had to stitch my skin back together."

The expressions on their faces were all wise and full of compassion and understanding. A boy named Clarence asked me, "Was someone chasing you with a gun?"

"No," I replied.

"Can we see your foot?"

I supposed I should have seen that coming. But there was no going back now. Dutifully, I pulled off my shoe and sock to show them the heavy-duty bandage. This unveiling of the foot led to a range of stories from the boys about injuries and incidents in their neighborhood that made my situation pale by comparison.

Later, I received a verbal reprimand from my superiors, not for the explanation that I gave to the boys but for the inappropriateness of exposing my naked foot and my wound to the students. But life—and my career—went on.

Best of all, I fell asleep that night at peace with myself, knowing that I had followed the courageous path that felt right.

Defining Courage

Courage is having the mental and moral strength to do the right thing for children. True courage exists at a very fundamental level. It would not be exaggerating to say that the success one has with each of the first seven leadership qualities is dependent on the courage to stick to one's convictions about those qualities and to see them through to the manifestation of tangible results.

Courage is much more than a single heroic moment of glory. More often than not, there is no glory in it at all. Rather, it takes the form of quiet diligence: the courageous acts are not always great, but they are courageous nonetheless. The leader who confronts a board of established so-called experts to stand up for what is right is courageous. The teacher who works day after day to promote the acceptance of a special needs child among the child's peers shows great courage as well.

Many people associate courage with impetuousness. But the knee-jerk brand of courage—while it has its place—merely brushes the surface for those who are serious about leadership in this field. For us, courage is a word with depth. It encompasses strategy and purpose. With intellect and sound logic, it helps us assess whether a challenge is best faced down today or approached again tomorrow when reinforcements are at hand and the lay of the land has changed. Courage gives us the strength to say what we are going to do, do it, and be willing to be held accountable for the results.

Bravado has no place within this leadership quality. Too many self-proclaimed leaders are fond of appearing brass and banging cymbals when, in truth, they lack the substance to back up their bold statements for change. A courageous leader has no need for smoke and mirrors. Those who dispense with them in favor of realistically observing and fully understanding the monumental challenges that lie ahead—yet who make the decision to strategically proceed toward that hard-to-reach goal anyway—are often the most courageous leaders among us.

Ultimately, courage is the core value that lies at the root of effecting change for children. Although there is immense potential in all of the concepts discussed in earlier chapters, that potential can only be reached by having the mental strength to turn good intentions into actions. Often, it is our courage that gives us that strength and compels us to take those actions in the face of daunting odds.

It takes courage to confront the status quo. It takes courage to argue with those in high, powerful places. People are afraid of change, and as such they may ridicule you and put up resistance when you present new ideas to them. It takes courage to present those ideas anyway.

As leaders in this field, we depend on courage to help us sustain our vision for a better, fairer world for children. We rely on courage to live out our mission to create that world. And when the challenges of building a more effective early education system become overwhelming, we fall back on courage, drawing on that inner strength. In the words of artist and author Mary Anne Radmacher, we look to that "quiet voice at the end of the day saying, 'I will try again tomorrow.'"

Courage at the Personal Level

Embodying courage at the personal level is a prerequisite for achieving success as a leader in early childhood education. But what does it mean for an individual to be courageous? Where do we draw the distinction between courage and its sister value of perseverance?

Personal courage happens on two levels. First, it involves cultivating an honest and unshakable belief in your core values so that you are able to stand strong in the face of any adversity. And second, it is about having the guts to look yourself in the mirror and admit that you are not perfect, thereby opening the door for your own improvement as an individual and as a leader.

To know what you stand for is to create a guiding star that is unique to you and your vision for the early education system. Our actions define us, and our values should always direct our actions. When we act on our own fundamental truths, we are really giving ourselves identity—not only from a personal standpoint but from an external one as well. Those who we purport to lead see the courage of our actions and respect us for them. This arrangement not only enables us to be even more effective as leaders but inspires those we lead to act courageously for what they believe in as well.

Being unshakable in your core values gives you the courage to say what needs to be said even when you anticipate that there may be negative consequences for you personally. The fact that you will be ridiculed for pointing out a problem or presenting a new idea does not dissuade you from bringing it to light. The possibility of becoming disassociated from your peers for your beliefs holds no sway over the beliefs themselves and does not hinder you from acting on them. When your values are more important than your job, you embody the courage required to be a truly effective leader in this field.

The second level of personal courage is being able to acknowledge your own flaws. As leaders, we often feel as though we are expected to have all of the answers. Yet this expectation is unrealistic. No one can know everything, and that includes leaders.

Being able to admit personal imperfection to yourself and others, however, is not always easy. Owning up to the fact that we don't know everything can make us feel weak and vulnerable. Ironically, having the courage to do just that actually succeeds in strengthening us. It takes courage to listen with a truly open mind to the ideas of others, but when we do, we benefit from the added perspective. It takes courage to acknowledge that we as individuals have more to learn, but doing so opens the door to personal improvement, thereby enabling us to make ourselves into the most effective leaders we can be.

In the end, the best test of courage at the personal level is your own state of mind at the close of the day. If you can reflect on your decisions with a sense of inner peace that you were true to yourself, then, regardless of whether those decisions met with the approval of others, you have acted with courage—and you can rest secure in the knowledge that you will be able to face any consequences that come of them with more of the same.

Courage at the Organizational Level

Whereas courage at the personal level has to do with self-examination and one-on-one interaction with others, courage at the organizational level involves taking on broad change outside of yourself.

It takes courage to see where organizational change is needed and then set out to change something that has been in place for decades. We all know programs that do what they do because that's the way it's been done. These programs haven't been around for as long as they have been because they are easy to disassemble. The people running them haven't been running them in the same tired, old ways for so long because they are quick to embrace alternate methods for improvement. Systemic change is required—and that takes courage.

Astute leaders seeking to make an impact on organizational and human fortresses know in advance that the odds are stacked against them. They know that the path to reform will be a struggle. Yet with the core value of courage to draw upon, these individuals tackle and conquer the challenges before them to effect bold and enduring change for children.

Communication within your own organization can sometimes also call for courage. Oftentimes, it falls to us to hold our colleagues responsible for their actions, even when doing so makes us unpopular. We are furthermore required to push beyond our comfort zones to help others resolve their differences, which can sometimes plant us in the middle of awkward or hostile relationships. Being able to deal with such situations effectively keeps them from undermining the common goal of the work at hand.

Bold and enduring change is not often effected using the same tools that one employs to achieve change at the personal level. One individual working alone is rarely able to accomplish sweeping and long-lasting results at the organizational level. Rather, the leader wishing to enact broad reform needs to use leverage.

Using leverage is not something to be taken lightly. With increased power comes increased responsibility. The potential for what can be achieved increases manifold, but at the other end of the scale, the severity of the consequences should things go awry increases as well.

One could look at it as going from little league to major league baseball. To lose a little league baseball game is to suffer personal disappointment. To lose the World Series is to incur the disappointment and even the wrath of thousands of supporters who had put their faith in your success. It takes courage to accept that kind of responsibility—and the potential consequences that come along with it.

It has always been a core belief of mine that children from underresourced communities should have access to the same quality programs that children from college-educated families have access to. When I set out to make that happen, the prevailing attitude was that the mediocre programs already in place were "good enough" for the children who were enrolled in them. People thought that I was crazy to try to transform the existing early childhood programs from good enough to great enough. They said it was ridiculous to provide high-quality programs for those underserved children who, they insisted, had neither the background to be able to benefit from my efforts nor the kinds of parents who would be willing to engage with the school and come to things like monthly meetings.

Facing down that kind of opposition was hardly a walk in the park. Nevertheless, I believed to my core in what I was doing, and before long I had convinced others to believe in my vision as well. My many years of trying to do the right thing for children has resulted in the establishment of an exemplary early childhood lab school at the University of the District of Columbia which was recently featured on the US Department of Education's website as a high-quality early childhood program. The majority of the children enrolled in the lab school meet the poverty guidelines for Head Start or our state child care subsidy program. In the end, my colleagues and I proved the naysayers wrong by having the courage to pursue our goal of creating dynamic, engaging, robust, and joyful learning environments for children from underresourced communities.

It takes true grit and courage to challenge the prevailing wisdom without losing direction or hope. However, if you seek to break through barriers and create enduring results for children, you must muster the strength and step up to the challenge. Figure out where you are going and be unrelenting in pursuit of that destination. Then decide which strategies you plan to use to disrupt the prevailing wisdom and turn it on its head in order to do the right thing for children. And finally, you must have the courage to remain steadfast in monitoring and protecting the breakthrough change that you have brought about.

Courage at the Classroom Level

I liken teachers to air-traffic controllers: they are constantly responding to the unpredictable and making on-the-spot decisions in the classroom. The inherent risks in that dynamic alone require no small amount of courage. Even so, those responsibilities only begin to brush the surface of what courage at the classroom level truly involves.

It can be difficult for us as leaders to admit our own fallibility, even to other adults. The courage it takes to permit children to see our imperfections is exponentially harder to muster. According to the old wisdom, any inch of uncertainty that a teacher exposes to his or her class is an excuse for those children to exploit the authority in question. It becomes an issue of control: the teacher must be in charge, and the students must follow the teacher's directions to the letter.

The first act of courage for the leader at the classroom level is to remove that "old wisdom" from the classroom setting. No teacher, regardless of age or experience, is able to truly thrive in an environment of perpetual rules and limitations. A tremendous leap of faith is required to release the preconceived notion that teachers must have total control over everything that children do from the moment they walk in the door in the morning to the time the buses and families come to pick them up again in the afternoon. Yet the incredible discoveries that come of giving children the freedom to explore will inevitably reward your courage tenfold.

Another facet of this core value at the classroom level is having the courage to learn from the children we teach. Even admitting that this is possible requires throwing out the old ideas of how the adult-child relationship—that of "I give the orders and you obey me"—ought to work, which is an act of courage in itself. Children come to us with a range of experiences and exposures, and as educators it is our responsibility to honor that. The realization that every child has something to teach you can be incredibly humbling. But, as with relinquishing control, the rewards of accepting this can be immense.

The combination of these two things—giving students freedom to explore and accepting that you need to learn as well as teach—comes down to building honest relationships with children, and that is what courage at the classroom level is really all about.

Back in the days of circle time, when I was a new teacher at my first school in Washington DC, I used to host touch-football games for my all-boys class in the park across from my apartment on Saturdays. At the time, I was new to the area, and as such I hadn't yet developed a social life. Ergo, why not extend the school week another day? I reasoned. I brought along hot dogs and Kool-Aid, and on the whole, the lot of us had a great time.

As the months went on, however, my social life inevitably did begin to develop. Fitting the Saturday touch-football games into the calendar became harder and harder. Finally, one week I decided that I needed a break from it all. However, I didn't want to hurt the students' feelings. So I made up an excuse.

"Boys," I said to the classroom that Friday afternoon, "Mr. Sykes will not be selecting a group to go with him to play touch football tomorrow because I have company coming over."

They didn't believe it for a second.

"Mr. Sykes, you don't have company coming over," declared eight-year-old Abdi, the unofficial leader of the class. "You're sick of us, that's all. You're sick and tired of us."

For a moment, I considered sticking to my fib. But I had been caught, and all of us knew it. I retraced my steps and opted for the honest explanation instead. "You know what Abdi? You're right. I don't have company coming tomorrow. But I'm not sick of you, either."

Immediately, some of the tension left the air. We were back on equal footing, and trust had been restored. Not long after, we came to a new arrangement that worked for all parties involved: instead of every weekend, we held our touch-football games once a month, and it was understood and accepted that I had a life beyond the classroom.

The courage to build an honest relationship with those boys served me well then, and the same principle has continued to support my leadership efforts—with both children and adults—ever since.

Cultivating Courage

To proactively cultivate courage in yourself and others, consider the following questions:

1. Do you have the courage to challenge yourself regarding your beliefs, actions, and motivations?
2. Do you have the courage to confront others regarding their beliefs, actions, and motivations?
3. Do you have the courage to accept new thinking and avoid uninformed thinking that does not achieve your goals?
4. Do you have the courage to stand up for children and do the right thing?

The Heart of Courage

Courage is the element that ties all of the other leadership qualities in early education together. It takes courage to advocate for human potential, to seek knowledge, to take stands for social justice, to dare to introduce fun into rigid models that have stood for decades, to make competent decisions in the face of outside pressures, to acknowledge and act on the importance of "selfish" personal renewal, and to persevere in the face of seemingly impossible odds. It takes courage to do the right thing for children—a mission that courage lies at the heart of.

People have a natural fear of and resistance to change. Yet by having the courage to stand by our core values and act on them even when the outcome seems bleak, we have the power to overcome tremendous odds on the path of building a better early education system that will provide better outcomes for young children and their families for generations to come.

EPILOGUE

So What's Your Leadership Story?

Storytelling is an old and revered tradition. Whether it takes place at a family gathering, around the campfire, at the watercooler, or in the teacher's lounge, storytelling can be an invigorating, transformative, and cathartic experience. Stories serve to provide us with a sense of time, space, and place. They are a way of being in the moment and recapturing the moment.

One of the great challenges for me in writing this book was to conscientiously reconcile my expressed core values with my observable core values. I was constantly checking my written story line against my living story line—a difficult task that requires the storyteller to confront truths, contradictions, and self-deceptions. However, the process of telling my story also allowed me to see where the gaps are between my perceived self and my actual self and provided me with the opportunity to align the two.

So I would like to invite you to tell your leadership story. I can assure you that you do have a story within you and that the process will serve as a powerful, transformational tool that will challenge and inspire you toward achieving your personal best. People are attracted to and connect with leaders who are willing to tell stories through authentic, real-world experiences. So give it a try. Follow the prompts below. And don't forget to be bold, be daring, and be courageous:

1. Describe your personal leadership attributes:
   - values
   - vision
   - passion

2. Explain your leadership perspective and experiences:
   - What are the leadership qualities that you value most?
   - How are these qualities observable in your leadership style?
   - What are the lessons you have learned from five to ten of your successes and failures?

3. Write a powerful story for each of your lessons learned.

4. Share your story with others and listen to theirs.

5. Keep writing, sharing, and listening, because each day is a new day along the path of your leadership journey.

INDEX

Maurice Sykes, director of the Early Childhood Leadership Institute at the University of the District of Columbia's National Center for Urban Education, has spent his career advancing high-quality early childhood education and advocating for educational reform and teacher professional development. Maurice formerly served as deputy superintendent and director of early childhood programs in the District of Columbia Public School System. He advised the US Department of Education on educational policy and programs related to urban school improvement and directed the Education Policy Fellowship Program at the Institute for Educational Leadership where he trained mid-career leaders. In 1997, Sykes was profiled as an Early Childhood Champion in a national study by the National Association of State Boards of Education and was elected to the Governing Board of the National Association for the Education of Young Children (NAEYC) in 1999. Maurice has written for numerous publications and has traveled nationwide inspiring and challenging schools and communities to do the right thing for children.